the ACTIVE WRITER

Michael Morris
Eastfield College

Kendall Hunt
publishing company

Cover image © Shutterstock, Inc.

Kendall Hunt
publishing company

www.kendallhunt.com
Send all inquiries to:
4050 Westmark Drive
Dubuque, IA 52004-1840

Copyright © 2012 by Kendall Hunt Publishing Company

ISBN 978-1-4652-0227-7

All rights reserved. No part of this publication may be reproduced, stored in a retrieval system, or transmitted, in any form or by any means, electronic, mechanical, photocopying, recording, or otherwise, without the prior written permission of the copyright owner.

Printed in the United States of America
10 9 8 7 6 5 4 3 2

Contents

CHAPTER 1 ACTIVE WRITING   1

You Want to Be a Better Writer   1
Competence and Beyond   3
What Is Active Writing?   3
The Basics: What You Need to Know
   (and Don't Need an English Class to Do)   4
Two Processes   5

CHAPTER 2 ACTIVE READING   7

Active Reading   9
Reading Your Assignments   11
Reading Your Teacher's Feedback   12
How Well Do You Know Your Syllabus?   14

CHAPTER 3 BASIC TERMS   15

Purpose   15
Audience   17
Context   20
Thesis and Development   20

CHAPTER 4 THE WRITING PROCESS   25

Prewriting   25
Planning and Drafting   35
Types of Drafts   39
Revision   44
Other Ideas for Improving Your Writing   51

CHAPTER 5 — DEVELOPMENT STRATEGIES 53

Narration/Description 53
Compare/Contrast 55
Examples/Illustrations 57
Cause and Effect 57
Classification/Division/Definition 58
Argument/Persuasion 59

CHAPTER 6 — ARGUMENT 61

The Basic Parts of an Argument 64
Appeals 67
Logical Fallacies 68

CHAPTER 7 — RESEARCH 73

Some Ideas for Gathering Information 76
How Can You Tell If a Source Might Be Useful 77
Checking Reliability/Credibility 79
Writing the Research Paper 81
Revising the Research Paper 83

CHAPTER 8 — DOCUMENTATION 85

Sample Entries 88

CHAPTER 9 — COMMON SENTENCE-LEVEL WRITING ERRORS 93

Sentence Fragments (frag) 94
Run-ons (ro) and Comma Splices (cs) 94
Wrong Word Errors (ww) 94
Verb Tense Errors (t) 95
Agreement Errors 95
Unclear Pronouns (pron.) 96
Quotation Marks (pron.) 96
Plurals (pl.) and Possession (poss.) 96
Titles 97

CHAPTER 10 **WRITING FOR...** 99

    Writing for Tests   99
    Writing for Other Classes   100
    Writing in the Work World   101
    Writing for Yourself   102

APPENDIX   **FORMS**   105

    Syllabus Contract   107
    Reading Quizzes   109
    Peer Review   113

CHAPTER 1

ACTIVE WRITING

Introduction: You Want to Be a Better Writer

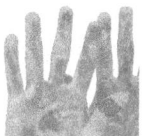

You probably don't realize it yet, but you really do want to write better than you do right now. Okay, you are not sitting there reading this thinking, "I wish I could write great poetry or even great essays for school." However, I have not met any student (and few outside of the school environment) who did not want better grades or the ability to put together good proposals for work or say more clearly what she or he wanted to say to a congressman and significant other.

Many people don't want to do the work of writing, and so they are not likely to want to do the work of learning to write well. I won't kid you: writing and learning to write better <u>is</u> hard work. But it has a number of benefits that make the struggle worth it.

Students who write well get better grades. This is a proven fact no matter what sort of instructor you get or what type of assignment you are asked to prepare. If you have to write an essay for a test, you are better able to clearly communicate what you were expected to learn. If you must do analysis of a poem, you have more tools at your disposal to get your ideas across even if you don't particularly like poetry. If you have to compare two products for an economics paper, you are better equipped to handle the project if you write better than you do now.

People who write well do better on the job. Employees who write well can usually handle projects involving writing with greater ease because they have more confidence in their abilities. For some people, even a simple e-mail is difficult to compose. There is even some evidence linking writing ability to promotions and earning capacity. Besides this, people tend to respect the person who communicates well, whether that is in oral or written formats. Heck, writing well may mean the difference between getting and not getting a job.

People who write well often do better at other tasks requiring thinking. People who write well are more confident when placed in situations where they must communicate themselves, even if few of the tasks involve producing text.

You might say that you write just fine, thank you very much, and don't need to improve. After all, you got out of high school and passed all the required standardized tests. Maybe you even got good grades on writing projects in the past.

I have taught developmental writing and worked as a tutor in writing centers. I'll bet I've had over a hundred students in those situations who have said the same thing.

Let me clear up a common misunderstanding. Your writing performance in the past does not mean you will do well in the future. I earned A's on most of the papers I wrote in college but still had much to learn when I became a technical writer. Then when I went to graduate school, I had to learn even more.

Further, every student needs to understand that *you are not in college to perform but to learn.* Most students come to the writing class with a certain amount of ability. They do the assignments, turn them in, and receive grades. Most students who do well praise themselves. Those who don't do well start placing blame: "My teacher doesn't like (or agree with) me" or "I'm just not a very good writer." They do not learn from the good work they have done or the mistakes they have made. Then the same thing happens each time they write.

You got into your college writing class because at some point you demonstrated that you had competence. This is the ability to do something. This does not mean you can do it well or even adequately.

Some people are gifted writers. This does not mean you cannot learn to write better. Some people struggle mightily to even bring their skill to barely passing. This does not mean you cannot be a better writer. I'm not an athlete, at least not in the sense that anyone would want to watch me. But if I worked at this, then I'd be better, probably not on a professional level, but at least good enough to keep in shape and enjoy myself.

The idea that "I'm just not a writer" or "I can't be a writer" is a myth. You *can* learn to communicate well in writing. And more than likely, you better.

I have mentioned grades. I don't plan to do so very often in this book, and please note that I make no promises about grades. I am not giving you a formula for getting A's. I'm sure I shouldn't say this as an English teacher, but you need to know that your grades are not important, at least not in the long run. Very few potential employers are going to ask you what grade you made in freshman composition. Your boss isn't going to keep you from working on an important project because you got a B or C on your research paper. You will prove yourself as a writer over and over in the real world. No one can attach a valid grade to that experience.

I also beg your indulgence a bit here. Part of this book is about steps you can take to improve your writing. Part is a philosophy of the art based on my own observations as a teacher and writer. Part is practical advice about the craft of writing from someone who has been there. Use this book in the way you most need to. You may read it "front to back" and take in the philosophy with the practice. You can skip either.

Hopefully I won't keep you too long from doing what the book is designed to help you with.

Competence and Beyond

There is a huge difference between competence and success. When one is competent, one has the ability to do a job and not much more. Your high school diploma or GED serves only to show others that you are competent in the subjects you were expected to learn. That is, you passed. They do not indicate your strengths or weaknesses. They do not demonstrate to employers or school officials that you have particular or special abilities. If you are working a temporary job, one that doesn't mean that much to you, you might not mind it if your boss writes on a performance review that you were "competent." However, if you were working in your chosen career, such an appraisal would not be satisfactory.

Presumably, if you graduated from high school or earned a GED, you proved that you were competent as a writer. But that competence may only mean that you have the ability to fill out a job application. As noted earlier, the good student wants to go beyond mere competence as a writer.

What Is Active Writing?

Most students enter college as passive writers and passive learners. They look for formulas and shortcuts to get through each course instead of looking at each class and each assignment as an opportunity to learn and grow. In fact, an ironic thing happens to most. They begin to see each course, particularly those outside their majors, as mere barriers, obstacles they must run through as quickly as possible, with no real connection to the jobs they are preparing for. What is ironic about this mindset is that in looking at your education this way, you actually can miss the opportunity to develop many of the skills you will need on that job and in your life outside of college, including skills in reading, writing, and critical thinking.

Passive writers expect writing to follow easy to define and follow formats. They cling to the five-paragraph essay and are confused by assignments which clearly will not fit that model. They rarely do more than look at the grade when a paper is returned, and so learn nothing from their successes or their mistakes.

The Basics: What You Need to Know (and Don't Need an English Class To Do)

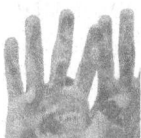

Even before you ever take a writing class or participate in your first workshop, there are two simple things you can do to become a better writer: **read** and **write**. Maybe that seems too simple. But just the practice of these two skills—skills you already possess to some degree—can help you improve. Keep in mind that writing and reading are physical and mental skills. The more you do them, the easier they become and the easier it is to grow.

Reading. One doesn't have to read only classic literature and textbooks for the simple act of reading to have a positive effect. Reading anything you are interested in not only increases your general comfort with the written language (vocabulary, grammar, mechanics) but also gives you tools and examples as you work to become a better writer. Reading material that challenges you in some way sharpens your thinking skills, something useful no matter what you do. I discuss how to be a more active and productive reader in the next chapter.

Writing. Practice makes close to perfect. The more often you do it, the easier the simple things become. The simple things are what you will build on to improve your skills and ability.

Once I read about a man who took up jogging for his health. At first, he couldn't finish a quarter mile without help. In a few years, he was running marathons. Maybe you aren't going to write the marathons of the world. But with work and persistence, you might find you are writing more and more impressively than before.

Tools. Every craftsperson has tools that are key to her or his success. I will discuss in more detail later some of these tools. But for now, keep in mind that a writer needs a dictionary, a thesaurus, paper and a writing utensil (even if you are using a computer), and hopefully access to a computer (even if you are writing with a pen and paper).

Two Processes

Many students are used to writing as one-draft wonders. Their process goes something like this:

Step 1: Receive the assignment, paying little attention to anything but the due date.
Step 2: Do as many things as possible to avoid actually confronting the assignment.
Step 3: Begin staring at the blank computer screen (or sheet of paper) the night (or morning) before the assignment is due.
Step 4: Either a) throw something together (somewhat related to the assignment) or b) plan how to ask the teacher for an extension.
Step 5: Turn the assignment in (or in extreme cases, drop the class).
Step 6: Forget about the assignment until it is returned with a grade.

Some students do add a seventh step where they either curse the instructor for not rewarding their "hard work" with an A or pat themselves on the back and sigh with relief at having survived another paper.

Because most students manage a degree of success[1] with this process, they often see this as the only way to write. Every semester, I hear "But I write best under pressure." Unfortunately, this is rarely true.

There are many writing situations where one has little choice but to write at the last minute or in a short amount of time, but rarely is this the case for major projects.

One of the most important ideas you should get from this book is that good writing is accomplished when it is seen as a series of steps or a process. For any number of reasons, these steps may vary in importance and difficulty depending on the project. Some steps will be accomplished one way on a project but differently on the next. Many times, the steps will seem pointless, but they will yield terrific results if taken seriously and practiced.

---

[1] And by *success*, I mean the student did not fail the assignment and/or was not required to do it over. You may have a different definition.

CHAPTER 2

ACTIVE READING

Reading is an essential skill, not only for survival in college classes, but for advancement in the working world. While you may not be asked to analyze Shakespeare or explain Jung's theories of the subconscious, you will be required to read information and instructions in a world that doesn't have SparkNotes to rely on.

Most students acknowledge the value of reading, but take as many shortcuts as possible in doing so (such as the above-mentioned SparkNotes), complaining that if the material doesn't interest them, they cannot do it or do it well. But in the real word, your interest in a subject does not mean you can avoid it, especially at work. Many students have survived classes in high school by doing little or no reading, and so they carry these habits into their college lives. And sadly, though much has been revealed to show a connection between those who read for pleasure and good overall reading skills and good grades, fewer and fewer students even read what interests them.

You must accept the fact that reading is essential and that your lack of interest in the subject cannot be used as an excuse for avoiding it. You cannot ask your professor for a special exam designed for students who don't like to read any more than you should expect your boss at work to only give you tasks that do not involve reading a manual or understanding written policies and procedures. (One might get such tasks, but few of them pay well or provide opportunity for advancement.)

So one of the first things a good student is going to have to do is get into the habit of reading. And it helps if you don't limit that reading to your class work. Students frequently complain that they do not have time for reading with all the work of school. However, even a few minutes of pleasure reading a day—a chapter of a novel or an article about a subject you are interested in—can have long-term benefits. Over time, you will find that reading tasks, even those in difficult subjects, may not be as tough as before. You may see connections with your reading assignments that help you remember concepts and ideas on exams. You will also, very likely, see your writing improve because you will have expanded your awareness of how the written word works.

Most students are inactive readers who apply the same techniques for reading for every reading situation. This doesn't work for a number of reasons. Consider that if you read something for pleasure, say an article in a magazine, you find it easy to do so because the subject matter is interesting and the writer has used language that is easy for you to follow. But if the writer uses words and phrases you do not understand, then the act of reading stops being pleasurable, so you stop. Now when you are asked to read a chapter in your textbook, you are likely to approach the material the same way. If it is difficult to read or if the subject matter is not of immediate interest, you don't want to keep reading.

But the significant difference between the article you picked up in a magazine and the chapter of the textbook is that nothing will change in your life if you put the magazine down or move on to a different article. Your professor, on the other hand, expects you to read that chapter and to understand the main ideas of it whether you want to or not. And even if you plow through the chapter, forcing your eyes to make contact with the page, you are not likely to remember much that will be useful. Just reading as one would any other item usually results in students getting a few paragraphs in and either giving up because they cannot comprehend what they are reading or counting pages every few minutes, wondering just how far they have to go.

At the beginning of each semester, many students purchase a handful of highlighters and steel themselves with hearty resolve to read everything that is assigned and thus be better students. They muster up enthusiasm and then open the first few chapters of their books coloring wildly anything that seems to be important. After a couple of chapters, these students usually give up because they have either highlighted half the material or nearly nothing, and either way do not seem to comprehend the material any more than had they just relied on the professor's lecture.

Highlighters have a place in reading, but they are not tools of active reading the way that many students have been led to believe. I recommend the use of highlighters during lectures. One should read actively *before* the lecture and highlight passages pointed out by the professor. This activity gives you an idea of what the professor thinks is important, but makes more sense when you are already familiar with the material.

Active Reading

In order to get the most from your reading experience, you need to adjust your process to fit your reading needs. Though you may be used to reading in front of a television or in areas that are filled with noise, you need to remove as many distractions as you can. If you need some sort of sound, try listening to music without words or very low so that the noise is there but not the distraction. Try to read alone and in a place where you are not so comfortable you are likely to get sleepy. Turn off the cell phone or at least put it away so you are not tempted to text or check Facebook.

Once you have set yourself in a good environment for reading, you will need a few tools. You should have a pencil and possibly some notebook paper (though you will see I advocate a more direct approach of annotating in the book itself). Again, put the highlighters away for now.

Pre-reading

Get a sense of what you have to read, not just by looking at the number of pages, but by skimming the material to see how it is laid out and organized. Are chapters divided into sections and subsections? What seems to be the purposes of pictures, illustrations, graphs, and charts? Are vocabulary words set in bold or italics?

In most textbooks, questions about the material can be found at the end of the chapter or passage or section. Students can help their reading by looking at these questions carefully before reading because they can help one focus on the important ideas or concepts. Good reading is usually about addressing expectations. Questions and a familiarity with the new words and ideas of a piece of reading put in your mind what to expect, and thus you are less likely to be lost trying to figure out what is important and what is not important.

It is also helpful, particularly when you have a good deal of material to cover, to section that material off so that you do not try to read it all at once. If you only have a couple pages to read, this is not necessary. However, most students are expected to read at least fifty pages a week per course. If you divide that material into smaller chunks, you can more efficiently read it all. Consider the following analogy. If you are just going down the street to pick up an item or two from the grocery store, you probably just get in the car and go. But if you are taking a long trip, you need to stop every once in a while to get gas, stretch your legs, and pick up a snack for the next leg of your journey. Reading large amounts is like taking that long journey. Try to read everything all at once, and you are likely to run out of gas or fall asleep at the wheel.

Reading for Content

As you read each passage or section, ask yourself a few questions about the material:

- What is the thesis or main idea of this passage?
- What points are used to support or develop this main idea?
- What key examples are there to help the reader understand the material?
- What are the important terms?

Underline the thesis or main idea of each section. Also try to write that main idea in the margin of your text, but do so in your own words. Write the points of support in your own words in the margin as well. You can later use these notes to construct an outline of the section. Circle or draw a box around any key terms or phrases—anywhere the author defines something for you. In addition, if you run into words you do not know or understand, mark them. Look up the words in your dictionary or in the glossary of the textbook if it has one, and write those definitions down as well.

I believe it is also helpful to write down personal reactions to your reading. Doing so helps you to engage the text and ask the important questions you need to ask in order to get a stronger understanding. Use symbols if necessary. For instance, if you read a paragraph and find parts of it confusing, try putting a question mark to remind yourself to ask about it in class. If something strikes you as funny or sad, draw a face or write the words "funny" or "sad." Consider asking the writer questions or making connections between the passage and something you have read or remembered from class or your experiences. Let me suggest you write your notes and annotations in the outside margin, and use the inside margin for any personal response. While this may seem (and feel) silly at first, you will find that you are able to focus on the material even more.

At the end of each major section or short chapter, look over your notes and try to write a short two to three sentence summary of what you have read. Write this in a prominent spot in the book, perhaps at the beginning of the chapter or section. Again, put this material into your own words, focusing only on the main ideas.

Review

Because you want to make sure your notes are accurate and useful, you may need to make some changes to them where necessary and put them into a format that you can use for study or for writing. You could create an outline of your chapter or a paragraph that summarizes the material in your own words.

Go over your notes before class so that you are familiar with what you learned and what you understand. Since you are likely to be doing this for more than one class, consider that you may find it difficult to remember material from several different courses until you remind yourself with your annotations.

As soon as you can, compare your annotations to lecture notes, highlighting passages the teacher focused on in class. Also make comparisons to any video or power point presentations you have had, and make corrections or new annotations where you either missed or misunderstood what you read. Ask questions when anything is unclear.

Prior to an exam or writing assignment, look through your notes, annotations, and ideas and put them into a legible and useful form such as an extended summary or outline. These can serve as basis for study as well as give material you can use for writing assignments. The act of writing is very powerful. It aids in memory and causes us to be more engaged in the subject. And you do not even have to be interested in that subject (but don't be surprised if getting a stronger hold on that subject doesn't peak your interest).

Reading Your Assignments

Over the years I have been teaching, I have noticed that one thing seems to stand out in student writing. Most students either do not fully understand the assignments they are asked to write or fail to follow all of the directions on those assignments. Thus, very capable people spend a great deal of time and wasted energy going in the wrong direction and lose points they could easily have earned.

Not only do some students wait until the last minute to write their papers, some actually wait until the last minute to read the assignment. This hurts their efforts immensely because then there is no time to figure out what to do or ask questions about directions that are not immediately clear.

Read all the way through your assignment without marking or pausing, just to get a sense of what it is about. Then go through again, marking key directions and noting words that give a hint about how to focus the assignment. For example, if your instructor tells you to *analyze* a picture, you don't want to summarize it and then just say whether or not you liked it. On the other hand, if the teacher wants your opinion about it, you need to be able to support that opinion with more than a summary and words like "interesting" or "humorous."

Instead of worrying about the length of your paper, consider using any length requirements as hints into how thoroughly you need to develop your points. If an essay is supposed to be 800–1000 words long, then you should assume the professor wants plenty of examples and explanations to make each point clear. If the professor is expecting you to limit your response to a single page, then you do not want to ramble around the subject but get to the point, develop it, and stop.

Of course, you need to look carefully at any research parameters. Is research required? Is it optional? Are there rules about the kinds of sources you are allowed to use? Are you expected to format that research in a particular way?

Reading Your Teacher's Feedback

Early in my teaching career, I was stunned to find out two interesting facts. First, most English teachers spend an average of twenty minutes per essay, marking, correcting, and making notes for improvement. Second, most students never read the notes their professors provide them. They look at the grade and nothing else. It is no wonder that there is such an adversarial relationship between students and professors!

Such actions (or lack of actions) have served only to increase the number of misunderstandings that students and teachers have about each other. When a teacher finds that her student has not made changes to a draft or continues to make the same mistakes over and over, it is hard for that teacher to keep from assuming that the student doesn't care and isn't interested in learning. When students "pour their hearts out" in essays and receive what they consider bad grades, they often assume that either the teacher doesn't like or agree with them, or that they are doomed to be bad writers all their lives.

Students need to remember that more than half of what they learn in a writing class takes place after the essay is written, not before. That most students do not read feedback says a great deal about why students get through such classes feeling as if they have not learned anything. In order to get value from your class, you need to read the feedback. Consider also that most students have made the same mistakes in writing since the seventh grade. That means they have not always grown as writers since that point. Now is time for change.

There are many reasons students avoid their teachers' feedback, not the least of which is not knowing it exists. Some have had some bad experiences or conflicted experiences regarding teacher feedback. Some are not aware of how to read that feedback since it may look like mere scribbles on the page. Teachers often make marginal notes about the content. They will sometimes draw arrows to indicate something about organization and write proofreading marks that look like abbreviations and little symbols. Also, some teachers have different expectations or mark according to different elements of the papers. For example, a history professor is not likely to correct grammar and punctuation errors. That doesn't mean there are not any mistakes or that several errors won't affect the grade.

Before we look at specifically how to read the teacher feedback, we need to change our mindset when it comes to this feedback. First, do not take notes personally. Your teacher is probably not interested in confirming your opinions or punishing you for having them. Your teacher's goal is to help you learn and may attempt that by forcing you to think critically about what you have written. So see these notes as an avenue for improvement.

Second, before your assignment is returned, go over it carefully and ask yourself what you would do differently if you were given another chance. When we finish a paper, we often have one of two feelings. Either we feel like what we have turned in is the greatest thing ever composed or that it is so bad that no one would ever willingly read it. But give your assignment a couple days to rest in your mind, and then look at it objectively. You may find ideas that needed better development or errors you missed when proofreading or running the spell check. You might even find that parts you originally thought were weak are not so bad after all.

Third, when you get the assignment back, try to ignore the grade as long as you can. Try to look at the notes not so much as a justification for the score you earned, but as a way to get a better score on the next assignment.

When you receive an essay back from your instructor, divide the notes into three sections. Remember that since readers think about what they read in three different ways, you need to make sure you understand what types of notes you have. First, identify those notes related to the content of your paper. These would be notes about your thesis and the development of your points. Second, identify feedback regarding the organization of your paper. Organization notes might include suggestions to move sentences or whole paragraphs. They may also refer to the placement of topic sentences or your thesis. Third, look for notes concerning your sentence-level writing. These will include the aforementioned proofreading marks and notes about grammar, punctuation, and sentence mechanics.

Identifying the categories of notes your teacher provides you should help you to pinpoint what has both hurt and helped you to communicate yourself clearly. Reading these notes should also give you an idea as to what you need to do on future assignments. Remember to focus on the specifics of your paper, not on your feelings or attitude about the subject matter. Also, make sure you understand the difference between correction and reader-based inquiry. Sometimes teachers will ask a question not so much for you to answer, as to show what might be going through any reader's mind as she or he looks at what you have written. Your teacher is trying to help you communicate more clearly with that reader.

Remember the goal of teacher feedback is to help you improve. Therefore, you should take this information and figure out what you need to do on future writing assignments. There is an old joke about a man who goes to the doctor and says, "Doctor, it hurts when I do this." The doctor replies, "Well, don't do that." You want to learn not only from your mistakes, but also from the things you do well. Students who do not read notes on their papers usually do not realize that the teacher may well praise something they have done well.

Understand that some feedback may not be clear for you right away, and tasks you need to work on may take more than one paper to appropriate into your writing. Content-related problems, in particular, take some practice to get used to. But do not allow those notes to sit there on the page. If you have done all this to read and comprehend them, and you still do not understand something, ask your teacher.

How Well Do You Know Your Syllabus?

Your syllabus is one of the most important documents concerning your course, and yet most students do not read it or even know where they can get the copy they lost after the first day of classes. While the syllabus may seem like the same old boring packet of paper, it usually contains valuable information that can help you not only keep up in the class, but also provide important parameters for writing that will save you trouble later on.

CHAPTER 3

BASIC TERMS

Purpose

One of the biggest differences between inactive and active writing is that active writing has a purpose. For so many students, there are only two "purposes" for writing anything: 1) to get through a class and 2) to express one's feelings.

But there is much more to real writing than this. Even if your main goal is pass a course, you may have several different reasons for writing something. For example, if you are taking an essay test, your purpose isn't just to pass, but hopefully to demonstrate to your teacher that you understand the material you were expected to learn. You also show that you can organize and discuss that material in a way that goes beyond mere memorization.

Sometimes people are confused about purposes, and so don't manage to do well or succeed in their writing tasks. For instance, if you were dissatisfied with a product you purchased and expected the company to refund your money, it would not be a good idea to rant for three pages about the "stupid" people who made the product or the "liars" who advertised the product. You would do better to calmly state what you expected, how the product failed to meet those expectations, and what you wanted, specifically, the company to do about the problem.

Consider another example. You want to use the family car for an outing with your friends, but your father has said no. Instead of discussing the matter and finding out what you can do to change his mind, you call him names and accuse him of being "unfair" and "selfish." He might well be unfair and selfish, but how often has calling people names ever gotten you want you wanted?

There are a number of purposes for writing something, and it would do the college student well to either understand or find a purpose that is greater than "getting a paper turned in so I can pass this class." And the various purposes for writing are not mutually exclusive of each other.

Inform. Sometimes we write to provide others with information we assume they do not have or something important about information they do have. If you are asked in chemistry class to explain the correct procedure for using a microscope, then you might have to imagine a student who has never used one (as opposed to your teacher who already knows) and go through the steps of using the device. You may have to go over any warning signs that would alert the reader when something is not working right or help them to understand the severe consequences of misusing the device.

If you were taking a government course, you might have to explain not only the concept of separation of powers, but do research on how the concept has evolved in history. If you were in a constitutional law course, you might be asked to look at Supreme Court decisions and actions by Congress or the President that have called the varied distinctions into question.

Express. Expression is the easiest purpose for writing to understand, and for some the hardest to do well. But it is one thing to express our feelings, something we are rarely asked to do in a college course, and another to express just what needs to be told or communicated to others. Believe it or not, it is when we express ourselves that we sometimes have to show the most restraint.

Let's say that you were upset about how a co-worker has treated you. Perhaps you feel your boss has not been fair in doling out work or in selecting people for choice assignments. Even though you may want to yell and scream about the situation, doing so may not help. You want to be honest about why the actions seem unfair and as rational as possible in expressing your feelings about the matter.

But this is not to say your feelings don't matter. They very much do. In fact, it may be easy to convince your boss (or his boss) that the actions were not fair, but without understanding the impact of those actions, he/she may not see a good reason to do more than say "I'm sorry," and continue doing what he/she always did. You may need to express that the actions have not so much hurt your feelings, but kept you discouraged from working to your potential or damaged the motivation you came to the company with.

Persuade. In many ways, all writing is persuasion. You want the reader to believe that what you say is true, even if you are just talking about your feelings or telling a story. Persuasion does encompass many elements, but note that the main purpose in persuasion is to get the reader to see your story, ideas, concepts, etc., are *believable*. One may sway others to one's position, but the goal is to get the reasonable person to see your points as reasonable and worth paying attention to.

An important idea to understand here is that your writing is not persuasive only because you believe something to be true or feel strongly about your subject. You can be "right" and still fail to convince anyone.

Entertain. You probably, unless you are in a creative writing course, will not be called upon very often to write something with the sole purpose of entertaining an audience. However, elements of writing to entertain are important to many writing endeavors. If, for example, you are called upon to write about a significant event in your life, you will not want that event to sound like every other similar event. I have had students who have made the most important moments of their lives sound incredibly dull, and they didn't need to be particularly creative in order to avoid such boring prose. Some needed more vivid description. Some needed dialogue. Some needed details to show why the story was not the same old thing written over and over.

Entertainment isn't always about being funny or telling a particularly sad story. Also, we should never assume that because the subject of our essay is about something serious (e.g., cancer or political beliefs), that our reader will automatically find the essay itself interesting.

But it is important to write the details and information in our essays so that it will keep the audience reading. Write, not as if your teacher has to read it because it is *his* job, but as if keeping his attention is *your* job.

Of course, in real, active writing, purposes overlap and build on each other. You might provide a lot of information in order to persuade your reader of something important. You may, in the process of expressing yourself, have the intent of entertaining your readers, so they will not just see your writing as a long rant with no connection to their own lives. At the same time, you want to be careful that you do not mix up purposes. For instance, if you merely express your anger at something, you are not likely to convince some readers to make the change you were expecting to.

Audience

Active writing keeps in mind that what we have to say is for an audience. Someone has to be the recipient of those words and so we must shape the words and sentences to best reach that audience.

Doing so is not without its trials. First, you have to get rid of the idea, fostered by many years of writing mostly for standardized tests, that the only audience you have is the teacher or someone behind a curtain that judges nothing but your sentence structure and spelling. In the real world, we write for real people, and even if we can only think of the teacher as the reader, that person is looking for more than correctly placed commas and proper pronouns.

Second, the active writer has to overcome the notion that what you have to say does not matter (or that it matters so much that any grade is a mark of the value of the idea, not the quality of the product).

In everyday life, those who are successful learn to adjust what they say to the person who is listening. If you talk to everyone like you are a rap star or like you are giving a talk at a U.N. conference, then you may feel good about what you've said, but you will not likely communicate your ideas, no matter how good they are. Further, you may have to adjust the information, tone, and word choice in order to get across clearly what you need to. The same is true with writing.

When we write something to our friends, it is usually via text, e-mail, or social media like Facebook. The people who are receiving our message, which is usually short, already understand enough about us that the use of shorthand and abbreviations or certain slang terms is not only acceptable, but expected. We are not asked very often to explain an idea or develop a point, often because the reader already understands what we mean. We are generally not taken to task for misspelling something because the goal in such writing is not to show how well we can use language.

However, these mediums are only part of the real world of writing. In the real world of writing, our audience may not be as clearly defined for us, at least not as clearly as our friends who share certain commonalities of language with us. Even people in similar roles might require different sorts of correspondence. For example, if you needed a day off while working at the local hamburger joint, you might have scribbled a note that read "Need Saturday off next week. Thanks, John." and left that on your boss' desk. But for a new boss, there may be a different protocol that requires something typed and more specific (Which Saturday? Why do you need this particular day off?).

As you might be able to see, audience is also tied to purpose. For example, imagine writing about a new romantic relationship. At the beginning of the romance, you would probably post something for your friends to read, and perhaps write something more personal about what you like about this new person (or what frustrates you about the relationship).

If you spent a lot of time with this person and your grades began to suffer, your parents might express their concern. You might find yourself explaining how this person has been good for you and how you promise to study harder. Or, if you were writing to ask for money, you might mention how your significant other has helped with a class in which you were struggling.

Later on in the relationship, you might see things as getting serious, and you have some concerns. So perhaps you contact your minister or a trusted adviser, someone who has experience and whose wisdom you trust to ask questions about the role of sex in a relationship or to express that you are worried about the drinking habits of your significant other, or to find out more about the religion she or he practices to consider its compatibility with your own.

We shall assume that you are not lying or leaving out important details in any of your writings. But you focus on the elements of the relationship you feel are necessary and base much of what you say on the people who are reading them and what you know about those readers.

Of course that makes sense when you are writing to someone you know about something you already care about. But what about writing for an academic audience?

In college classes, the audience is oftentimes not clear. You are just told to write a paper. And for many of you, years of standardized testing has conditioned you to see the audience as merely the teacher or some teacher-like figure who is judging esoteric qualities in your writing. And certainly it is difficult, no matter what the assignment tells you, to get away from the idea that the person reading the paper will be a teacher. It matters most, we assume, what the teacher thinks because it is she who will grade the assignment.

But we need not let this problem get in the way of envisioning a bigger or broader audience. This way, when we compose and develop our ideas, we have something to shoot for more than getting a certain number of words written.

If an audience is not provided for you, it is helpful to imagine writing for your class. Think of your reader as someone who is smart enough to be in college but in the process of learning many things. These are readers who do not always think alike, so not every appeal will work on them. These are readers who need certain points fleshed out so they can be convinced or so they can "see" what you see as you think about what you write.

I often tell students, "What is clear in your head is not clear in mine. It is your job to make it so." Thus, you need to avoid making assumptions about what they know or do not know about your topic. You need to also avoid writing down to them, as if everyone reading your work is incapable of understanding anything not written in academic baby talk.

Sometimes an audience (or certain information about an audience) is implied. For example, in a literature course, a student might be asked to analyze a short story. The student would do well to assume the reader is familiar enough with the story that a detailed plot summary would be unnecessary. A short summary of the narrative would suffice. However, if a point is being made about a character or something in the setting, the student writer would do well to quote or refer to something very specific in the story to support the point.

Let's say, however, that you are writing a report for a chemistry class on an experiment you were called on to perform. You would not need to define some of the terms common to scientists (unless your professor instructed you to), but only to tell what you did and describe the reaction and conclusions you came to based on that reaction. On the other hand, if your readers are not science students or teachers, you may have to explain some of those terms or address what the conclusions mean for people outside the laboratory.

Context

No writing assignment is the same. Because of this, active writers adjust what and how they write to those situations. Context covers a variety of elements from how much time you have to write to the amount of research you are expected to do to special circumstances of your composition.

In some ways, your essay's context is very much about the rules and expectations of your project. Is the writing to be done in a timed setting in class? Are multiple drafts expected? How many words does the professor expect or are you limited to a single page? Will collaboration be involved? What documentation style does the professor require?

But in other ways, context is about everything not covered in the parameters. You could make a proposal to your boss with a simple e-mail, but may find it better to make an organized and developed report stating your case with facts and figures. In a chemistry class, you might be asked to write a report of an experiment using a particular format. Just writing "what happened" would not be sufficient. Some teachers allow you to use the textbook on an essay test, while others may expect you to study and remember the pertinent information.

It is important to have a clear understanding of the context of your writing assignment because you need not only to budget your time and energy, but understand what your professor or supervisor expects you *not* to do. Many a student wastes valuable personal resources chasing after material they do not need or that only gets in the way of the goals of the assignment.

Thesis and Development

Your **thesis** is what your entire essay revolves around. It is not the subject of your paper, but the main point you are making about that subject.

For most academic essays, this statement will be positioned in the first paragraph of the essay, typically the end of that paragraph. Remember that an introduction will serve two purposes: to engage your reader or get them interested and to tell the reader where you are going or what your paper is about. This last purpose is achieved with a well-written thesis statement.

You want your thesis to be specific and clear. Vague and general points do not really give you room to write and do not tell your reader very much about what you want to say. Consider the following examples:

Baseball is my favorite sport.
I enjoy baseball because it is fun and exciting.
I have learned a lot playing baseball.
Baseball has taught me valuable life lessons.
Playing baseball, I have learned the value of working together for a common goal, how to deal with attacks to my character, and how to think quickly in a crisis.

Each of these statements tells what a paper might be about, but you should be able to see that each one gets more and more specific. The more specific your thesis is, the more you will have to say about your subject. In your drafts, a specific thesis will help you to focus your thoughts and development.

There are times when a thesis is unstated, particularly with essays that are mostly narrative. In this case, a reader should easily be able to figure out the main point or purpose of the essay.

Problems to Avoid with Thesis Statements

Avoid the vague and the general. A sentence like "Baseball is fun" or "My graduation was the most important day of my life" do not tell your reader where you are going in your paper and are bland.

Avoid preaching, moralizing, or other grand statements about the universe. Unless the purpose is to talk directly to the reader about an action that needs to be taken, you have no business telling the reader what to do. Lose sight of your purpose and it is easy to assume that telling the story of your car accident is also where you inform your readers that they should not take life for granted. Such a story, if compelling, will allow a reader to make that determination for herself. But if the real purpose is to show how *you* changed after an accident, then focus the thesis in that direction.

Avoid announcing your intentions. Statements that begin "In this essay, I will . . ." and "This paper is about . . ." only remind your reader that he or she is reading an assignment. Make it your goal to write so well that the reader would have wanted to focus on your ideas. Also, such constructions make for stale reading.

Development

Your body paragraphs will support and develop your thesis statement. In each paragraph or each major section of your essay, you are likely to have sub-points, often called topic sentences, which will point back to that thesis. Each of these topic sentences will need to be developed in some way, depending a great deal on your purpose and your audience. These developmental strategies are addressed more specifically in Chapter Five, but the basic forms of development are listed here.

Narration is simply telling a story that is appropriate for the purpose of the paper. Sometimes that story forms the crux of the essay. Sometimes a brief anecdote is used as an example to help prove a point.

Description involves using sensory and concrete details to give your reader a stronger sense of what people, places, and objects look like, sound like, etc. Description is not just for stories, but also helps the reader in other ways, such as in process writing or comparisons/contrast development.

Comparison requires the writer to focus on significant similarities. When you explore significant differences, you are using *contrast*. Each of these can be used to prove a point or to highlight different processes.

Examples are used to illustrate a point or idea. Sometimes these are stories, but sometimes they are sets of facts that help the reader to understand the idea. This is one of the most common ways to develop ideas.

Process writing is about telling your reader how to perform a task or showing your reader how something is accomplished. The first type of process writing usually involves detailed instructions. The second type requires explanation of how something works.

When tracing *cause and effect,* you are looking into a chain of events and how each event relates to others. Here it is important to look carefully at all the details, leaving nothing out of your exploration of the events. Often, students make assumptions that hurt their efforts to persuade or communicate effectively.

Classification means to put things into categories your reader can understand or needs to understand. An idea can be made clearer by showing clear distinctions about groups. With *division*, you distinguish things in one group from another. Here one focuses on the specific distinctions between groups.

Definition is where you explain what something means. That may not mean only providing a literal or dictionary definition, but explaining a term or concept.

Argument consists of the writer making a claim and providing reasons to support that claim. There are many different elements to argument, which are discussed in Chapter Seven. But sometimes a writer will need to make a case for something in the middle of a paper so that the reader can understand the thesis. In that way, one might say that all writing is argument.

I hope you can see that while you may have written essays in the past which focused on only one of these modes or rhetorical strategies, writing in the real world often involves combining strategies or using different ones to suit different purposes and different audiences.

Conclusions

If you think of your introduction as the first impression a reader gets of your ideas, then you can look at the conclusion as the last image of those ideas. It is, in a way, like the parting handshake at the end of a meeting. The points have been made and developed, but a wrong move here can turn the reader off.

I cannot stress strongly enough that your conclusion should not be a rehash of your main points. This is insulting to your readers because it tells them they are not smart enough to remember what you have just told them. It also is lazy writing.

You want to end your paper with a bang, or at least with the same energy and fervor found in the body of your essay. You want to give your readers something to hang all those ideas on that sticks in their minds.

Avoid the following in your conclusions:

- Any of the problems that also plague poor thesis statements and introductions.
- Restating the introduction.
- Bland statements or rambling about the general subject.
- Introducing a new idea.
- Changing the point of view from informing the reader to telling the reader what to do.
- Being dull.

Consider instead:

- Connecting to something in the present world that is affected by your main idea.
- Providing an anecdote that puts your main idea into context or shows its importance.
- Explaining why the main idea is significant for the reader (without using second person) or whomever is most affected by the idea.

Chapter 4

THE WRITING PROCESS

Prewriting

The two most often skipped steps in the writing process are prewriting and revision. For a variety of reasons, most students do not see the value of these essential elements to good writing. Students usually try to write an essay off the tops of their heads, trying to fit the old five-paragraph formula or rambling until good ideas just come to them. Having put together a draft of sorts, after waiting until the last minute and wasting a lot of time looking at the blank page or screen, some students will run a spell check or "go over" the paper before turning it in.

Because the college student has passed most writing assignments with this method, he or she assumes that this process "works." But just as success breeds success, false success breeds false success.

What is wrong with being a one-draft wonder? For one thing, this mentality assumes that ideas just "come to us" and that only gifted writers can do well. This gives the student a convenient excuse to not work on improving, and remember that, in the real world, employers do not ask if we are gifted. They just expect results.

Another problem is that the more complex the writing task, the more difficult such an approach is likely to be. While most college freshman can pull together a quick five-paragraph formula essay that got by in high school, such writing is not typically found in college courses or in real life. We may be expected to look at things differently and perform writing tasks we are not used to, even to add reading, research, or collaboration to the process. We usually need to spend a good deal of time developing potential topics and then narrowing to a specific point because the general essay no longer suffices.

Even if you are successful, in the sense that you pass the assignment, you are not likely to do your best work. Sure there are times when we get "inspired," and everything we want to say just falls into place, but those instances in college writing and in the real world are few and far between. And your professors and employers are not likely to wait around for inspiration to strike you. So you do what you can and get the project in, but how much better would that paper have been had you taken more time at the beginning to explore your options and possibilities?

Some students claim they write best under pressure. However studies demonstrate this is not so. Without taking time to work out ideas and plan essays, writers sometimes fool themselves concerning the quality of their prose because they have felt the adrenaline rush of working fast and furious at the last minute. Thus, it may look good to you upon completion, but when examined in a critical light the material may well be lacking in several ways. In the meantime, you have added more stress to what is already a difficult and stressful task.

You might say, "My teacher isn't going to look at any notes I make before I write. The teacher only cares about the final product." This is true for most students, even in writing classes. However, why spend so much time staring at a blank screen that tells you nothing when you can work through a variety of ideas and directions on paper?

There are several techniques that students can use to generate ideas and material for writing. Each works differently and in different circumstances. If you try each technique several times, you will find that some seem to work better for you than others, but don't assume the others don't work. Sometimes the best way to deal with writer's block is to try a prewriting technique that you haven't done before or have not used much.

As noted in Chapter Two, it is imperative that you read and understand your assignment carefully before you begin. Doing so will ensure you don't have so many false starts and make it much easier to make prewriting work for you. Also, it is important that you turn off that mental censor during the prewriting phase. That little voice inside your head that says that something is a stupid idea or that a thought is "wrong" is the voice that stifles your ability to think creatively and come up with good ideas. Ignore that voice until the revision stage when it is time to refine and polish what you have written. Your goal is to engage your mind on the subject and the assignment at the same time you record your engagement. As you plan, you can determine which material is worth pursuing or keeping and what doesn't work for the purpose, audience, and context of a particular assignment.

Brainstorming. One of the easiest and most common forms of prewriting is brainstorming. Here one simply takes the general subject and lists as many ideas and topics as one can come up with. It is a good idea to start with the general subject or a goal from the assignment to make your first list.

Stories:
graduation
first car
first accident
breaking up
Grandpa's funeral
cancer scare
trip to church camp

Once you have a list of potential topics, you can pick those that seem to stand out to you, either because they interest you or because they seem to best fit what the assignment should be about. Pick more than one good topic and then make another list using a key word from the assignment. For instance, if the assignment asks you to tell a story and you list several events in your life, you can pick one that you like and then start brainstorming about descriptive details.

first accident
just got licence
parents' warnings
friends not sitting still
no one hurt
sunny day
hot outside
going to pool
big dent in my side door
was too shaken up to drive
Dad chewing me out, later calm

From your two lists, you can even narrow the focus by making a new list, one that consists of people the story affected, how they were affected, and how the event has changed you.

people/effects
father
mother
Kayla
Shelby
policeman
angry dude I hit
won't let people drive with me who aren't careful
had to pay for damages
took a long time to feel comfortable driving

While some of the details generated using brainstorming will be not be used, and these lists are certainly not a developed essay, you can start to outline or plan the paper, at least in a basic form, from these notes. Also, should you find after beginning to plan or draft that the topic you have chosen or the direction of your paper isn't going to work, you still have some other material to work from. So you aren't really starting over.

Freewriting. Freewriting is, in one sense, exactly what it sounds like: writing that goes in whatever direction you want it to, with nothing to stop the writer, even if she or he is off topic. But it is really more than just jotting stuff down off the top of your head. Here you should take your general subject and, for a short period of time (I recommend no more than five minutes until you have done it several times), write what comes to mind, trying to focus on your subject, but allowing yourself the room to roam around.

Freewriting works best when the writer has a specific subject or topic to work with. For example, if your assignment is to write about a significant event, you might write down a phrase like, "What happened when . . ." or "I remember my. . . ." It can also help to start with a topic you have come up with during a brainstorming session. Then set a timer and just go. Write without worrying about grammar or spelling or even neat handwriting (though this can be done using a computer). If you cannot think of something to write, then write, "I can't think of what to write" or something like it until your mind unblocks. When the timer goes off, finish the thought you were working on and stop.

Now, you will likely have a paragraph of words that go in different directions, and perhaps only some of the material will seem on topic. But go through and highlight what is on topic or related to the assignment.

I remember when I had my accident ==I was very scared== after, ==my dad kept saying I could have been killed== and I

yelled at him to leave me alone which is not really what I
wanted. I can't think of something to say now. Oh yeah,
there was a lot of noise and the radio was going. what was
that song we were listening to that Kayla just had to had up
i can't remember i can't remember i wish my hand didn't
hurt doing this. that was a scary accident and i'd even been
in one before, but that was not me driving and I think the
boy next to me is not doing this right i wish he'd quit
humming.

Many students are surprised at the ideas they come up with using freewriting. It works typically because one does not let the inner critic get in the way and block the gates of imagination. Students frequently report to me that they end up writing things they didn't know were in their heads. And while lots of the material is useless, and one should not use a freewriting exercise as a part of the paper, even if one good sentence or idea comes from that five minutes of work, it can be the gold you need to start a mine.

Also, for many students, an exercise like freewriting may feel uncomfortable or like a waste of time, particularly if nothing comes of your five minutes of labor. But I have had students who start with freewriting because even when they do not get a good idea to write about, they do relieve some of the stress of starting a new writing project, and that alone makes the effort worth the trouble.

There are a number of things you can do with the useful material you get from this technique. You can do some brainstorming to list ideas. You can take a sentence you generated and make it the center of a clustering exercise or ask the journalists' questions about the subject. If you come up with several good ideas, you can put them in a chart and see what you would need to develop one or more of those ideas.

Clustering (Mapping). Clustering is a form of visual brainstorming. The goal, however, is to try and move from one general topic or idea to more specific ideas or details.

Let's say that, with the narrative exercise, you decide that a good topic might be to write about getting your first car. You could then look at the different elements of such a story. Of course there would be the narrative itself, the "plot," or what happened. But what needs to be described? Probably the car itself and the feelings of anticipation in obtaining it or the sounds and sights on the test drive. Each of these objects or parts of the overall story could be a spoke coming from the original "wheel" in the center.

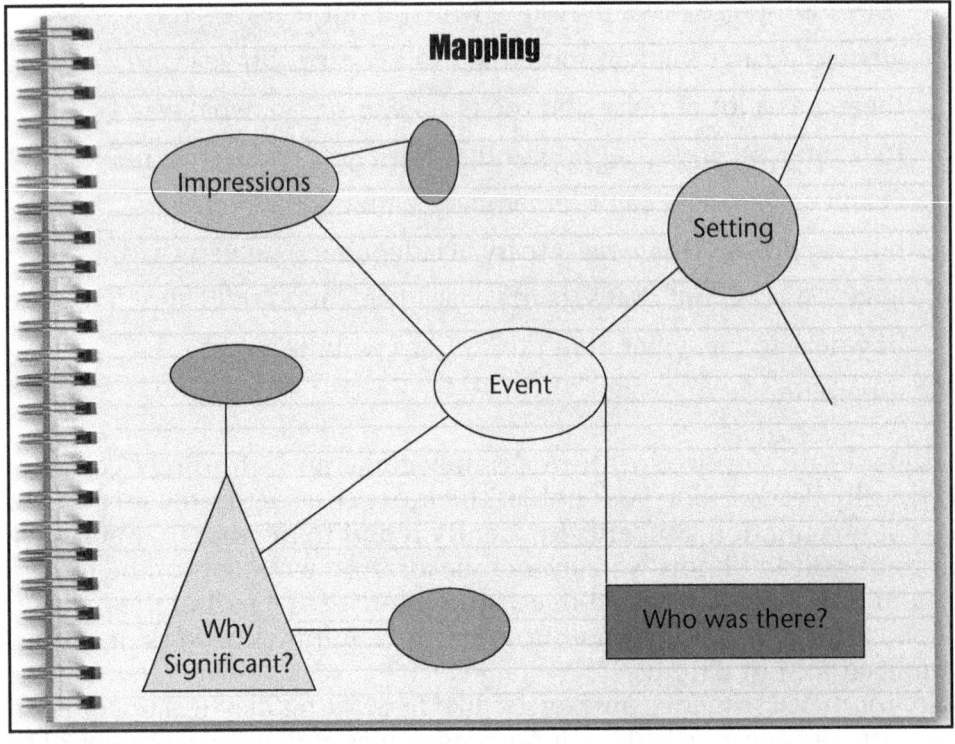

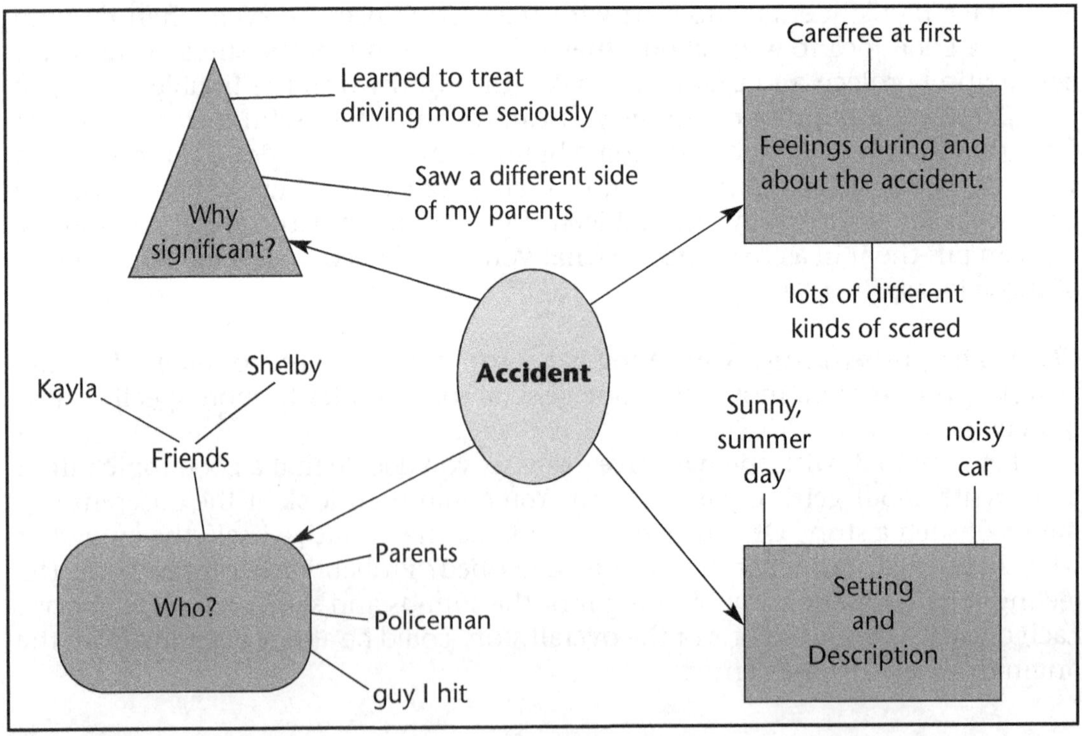

Once one cluster has yielded different ideas for your paper, you can take one of those ideas and make that the center of a new cluster in order to develop the details and ideas you need for different parts of your paper.

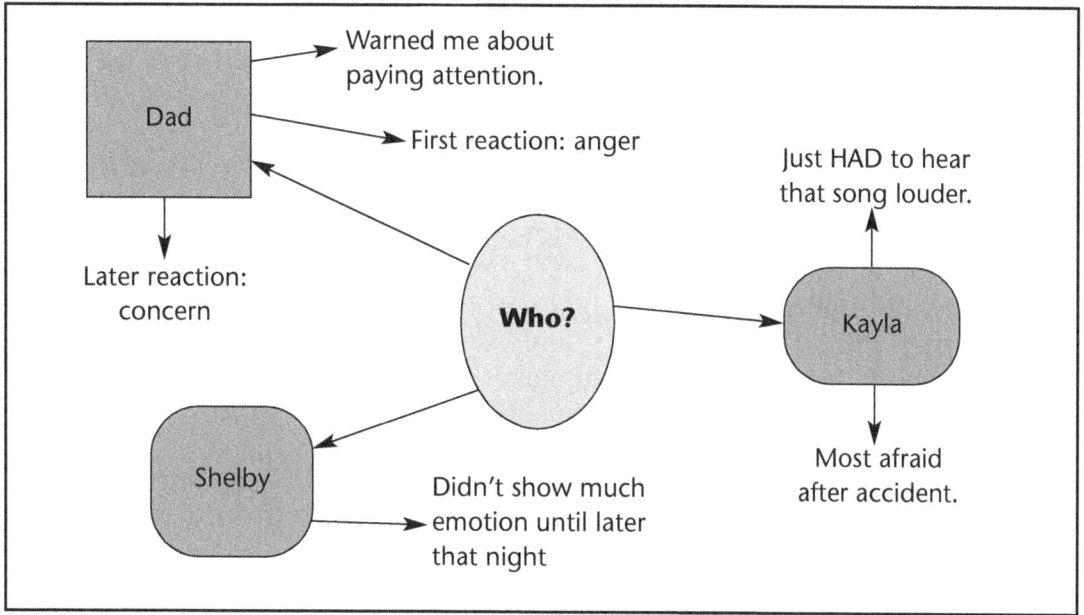

Clustering, like other prewriting techniques, can also be used to help you during writer's block. Consider taking the subject of a section of your paper you are struggling to write, put that subject in the middle of the page, and draw spokes from it where you can explore different ways to develop or explain your subject.

Journalist's Questions. One of the most common ways to explore a topic is to use the simple questions used by journalists. A news story typically has something that addresses all or most of the following:

- Who?
- What?
- When?
- Where?
- Why?
- How?

Not all of these questions may fit every assignment. However, remember that prewriting is a way to get started and not necessarily to fill every inch of the essay. Answer the questions as thoroughly and with as much detail as you can, even if at first the material seems to be off the topic. You can always reshape or omit ideas that don't work for your purpose.

Consider just a few questions we could ask about the narrative assignment we considered earlier:

- Who was involved in the story? Who is an important "character," and who is just a side player? Who was affected by the event that is not in the story?
- What happened? What objects are significant to the story? What could have been different?
- When did this take place (time of day, point in my life)? When did I come to a realization about the events?
- Where did the story take place? Where were other important people when this happened?
- Why did this happen? Why did I (or others) react to these events as I did? Why is this event important to me?
- How did this event affect me or make me different? How have others acted since this took place? How do I expect to move on after this event?

It can also be useful to ask the journalist's questions of your assignment, particularly if you are struggling to understand all of the parameters. Sure, the question "Why do I have to do this assignment?" has the easy answer of "Because I'll get a bad grade in the course if I don't." However, you might consider seeing how these questions can be addressed in terms of your purpose, audience, and context. Remember that when you have a clear handle on those concepts, you can more easily make the decisions necessary to compose a strong essay.

One reason the journalist's questions work for so many writers is because readers subconsciously ask those questions when they read, and thus it helps the writer to think like the reader, an important element of strong writing. Once readers get hooked on a story or an idea, they have gaps that are often represented by these questions. Good writers will fill in those gaps.

Journals/Notebooks. A perhaps more advanced form of prewriting also happens to be a good study habit: keeping a journal or notebook of information and thoughts about different elements of your course. This allows you to take ownership of what you study and make your assignments more interesting.

A reading journal can help you to keep track of what you have read and also give you the space to work out how material you read in your textbook or in doing research is connected to assignments you have to write. You can summarize chapters and articles, but also lectures and films you encounter, even in other classes. You can take a few minutes to jot down your impressions of a story you read for class or ask yourself what is important about a chapter in your textbook. You can even write about frustrating or difficult passages and find good ideas for future writing or research. As noted in the chapter on reading, even those more "personal" ideas force our minds to be engaged in the subject, so we think about it when we most want to put it away.

Consider keeping a journal either in a notebook or online. Start by taking each passage you read for your classes and writing a short summary. Make it a single paragraph where you merely hit the highlights of what you have read. Then try writing another paragraph or two, a personal reaction: What was interesting or boring about it? What do you think your professor is going to say in class about it? How is this like or different from something you read for another class? What was confusing or troubling for you? Answers to these questions may well give you ideas for papers, or at least give you something to discuss in class.

One of the best things to do in a journal is to constantly ask yourself about how what you read or learn in class is connected to the papers you have to write. This means you have to keep looking at what you are expected to do and engaging your mind on the task instead of ignoring the project until it is nearly due.

Charting. Another method of prewriting that seems to work for many students is charting. Here, one creates columns to help fill in the parameters or expectations of an assignment. For example, let's take the narrative paper mentioned previously. To tell a story, one needs to have particular plot points. Thus, those can be listed on the left side since this will make up the bulk of the essay (not counting the introduction and conclusion). Then columns can be created to help you put in other necessary elements of the story.

Charting

	Sensory details	Impression	Dialogue
Plot point 1			
Plot point 2			
Plot point 3			
Plot point 4			

Consider that for another paper, you can substitute the plot points here with specific sections that might make up an essay. Note, for instance, how we might chart a potential argument:

Section	Main Idea	Research	Examples	Explanation	Other information
Background					
Point 1					
Point 2					
Point 3					
Point 4					
Counterargument/ Refutation					
Concession/Common Ground					
Application					

Certainly you can have more than one item for each section, but this may give you an idea of how to make sure each part of your paper has what it is supposed to and also help you structure the body of the essay as you come up with new ideas.

The main advantage of prewriting is that it helps you engage your mind more directly with your task as you generate ideas and material. Nothing is set in stone, and you will find that even after doing a lot of prewriting some ideas come as we draft. We sometimes find that something that seemed good when we started is not so good as we write. That's alright. You may find that an idea you came up with and rejected at first might be worth pursuing. Sometimes material you reject for one essay will work well for another. Thus, you should not get rid of the prewriting, even those rejected ideas.

Also, you should try each technique several times before you decide it doesn't work for you. For example, you may find that you are not comfortable doing freewriting or that creating a chart doesn't seem help you come up with anything. And that may be true in most cases. But then when you have difficulty with what has usually worked, one of those techniques could be just what you need.

Because of this, remember that what I have been calling prewriting isn't limited to just before you plan and draft your paper. These techniques are also useful when you are experiencing writer's block as you draft a particular section of your paper or in helping you in revision when you realize you need to further develop or reshape a section that needs work.

Last, I strongly recommend using more than one technique for each writing project. Let one grow out of another. For instance, many students find it useful to do some freewriting first and take the ideas that come from that activity as the center of a clustering exercise. Others will brainstorm about topics they have explored in their journals. The main thing is to make it work for you so you don't waste precious time and energy telling yourself that you can't think of anything to write about.

Planning and Drafting

There is not really a single "right" way to draft an essay. Many students have learned a process in school or have become comfortable with a method they have used, either of which has seemed to be successful, and so decide that no matter what, that is how the essay *must* be written. Some have never really learned a formula, and thus stare at a screen or blank piece of paper until something pops into their heads or they just write whatever they can think of until something takes shape or until the word count is fulfilled, whichever comes first.

Often, the method that works in one context does not work in another. For instance, if you are a student who likes to do some research about a topic before writing, you'll find yourself in a pickle when taking an essay exam. Sometimes what worked before does work in what seems to be the same writing situation. That old five-paragraph formula, where you generate your ideas after you come up with three points to make, may not be as useful when the teacher expects each point to have a lot of development or when you can't come up with three good points.

Before I get into different methods for composing a draft, I want to make a few points about preparing to write and the role the draft plays in the whole process. (Remember, it is only part of that process.) Also, note that this chapter is only about first drafts. We will discuss the other drafts in the section on Revision.

Environment: Removing Distractions and Building a Space for Work

Even seasoned writers need a proper environment to be successful in writing. And many students make mistakes about what they need and what they do not need. Unless you are writing about something you are watching on television, you do not need the television on or even in the room. Just being in the same place as the television proves, for most, to be a huge distraction. While you might be aware of how much you need to finish your paper, most would rather be watching almost anything than writing.

The same can be said about the computer, which is tricky since most writing has, at some point, to be done on the computer. For this reason, I favor using as low-tech an approach to the first draft as possible. When composing something short (three paragraphs or less), I usually write the first draft by hand. Anything longer, and I try to employ WordPad instead of a more complex word processing program. This keeps me from getting worried about grammar and spelling because I don't have a little squiggles popping up every time I mistype something. I don't concern myself with formatting because I know that in a later draft, I will import my file into Word or another program and straighten all those issues out. It also keeps me from worrying about how long what I write is, since the word count isn't available to me. For many students that alone is a huge distraction, because they are more concerned about getting a certain number of words down than developing their great ideas.

Another issue in using the computer is the Internet. Just as it is tempting to watch TV, most of my students would rather be checking Facebook or playing a game instead of doing the work of writing (and it is work!). Sometimes students get stuck on some part of the paper and decide to do a Google search (or worse, Wikipedia!). This sort of action actually can bring many more problems than it can solve.

I recommend avoiding listening to music unless it is without words or at a very, very low volume. That takes some getting used to for most people because they have done it for so long that it seems to be part of who we are. It is like lighting a cigarette after a meal. Just because you are used to it or it feels good does not mean it is a good idea.

Thus, it should go without saying that writing, especially first drafts, should probably be done in a place where you can be alone for a significant length of time. Our friends and family are more important than any stale English assignment, and though they may even appear to be helpful, we need to get through that first draft on our own.

This is not to say we should not have an environment that makes us comfortable, just not too comfortable. Writing should not be a prison. Good lighting and temperature are often ignored, as well as the type of chair or table one works at. Sure, some elements are outside of our control, but we need to control as much of the environment as possible, or the environment controls us and keeps us from doing well and, in many cases, from just plain doing the work.

Preparation

I cannot stress enough the value of preparing well for writing. For some, this takes the form of a very detailed outline. Sometimes it is merely a matter of jotting down key points you need to pursue in the essay. (Remember the word *essay* comes from the French verb *essayer,* which means "to try.") For rather complex projects, especially those that involve research, I like to create a chart that helps me to intersect what I need to accomplish, what I have come up with on my own, and any research I have found or interesting quotes that pertain to my points.

Many students try to write cold, even after doing considerable prewriting to help them come up with ideas and narrow the focus of the writing project. But that is like stretching and then stopping to have a bag of doughnuts before going jogging. The mind has something to work with but no real direction. If all goes well, however, the prewriting will lead to good planning.

Many students are often taught to make a **formal outline** in school. Usually this takes the form of section headings after Roman numerals with Arabic numbers getting assigned to subheadings (or paragraphs) and even smaller Roman and Arabic numbers attached to specific details or development within paragraphs.

This sort of planning works well for some students, but not for others. If you have a general idea of what you need to say, but need to organize your thoughts into a reasonable order and figure out the best way to develop each major idea, this is going to work for you. However, I have had many students report to me that when they were in high school, they did the assigned outline *after* writing the paper, so as to avoid getting points counted off. I was just such a student. And as I'll note in the section on revision, this sort of outline is more useful for some writers during that stage because it helps the writer to test elements of the paper that they might not see otherwise.

An advantage of the formal outline is that when it is well done and carefully thought out, the writer has a much easier time writing and organizing a rough draft and usually needs fewer revision drafts to get the paper into good shape. A disadvantage is that for most people, the formal outline gives students a boxed-in feeling, and when, during the course of writing, a good idea comes along, the student might ignore it because it isn't on the outline. Conversely, if the writer sees that one idea isn't really working as she drafts, she might not abandon that part of the essay in favor of something better. Keep in mind that writing is a messy process and that nothing needs to be neat and pretty until the final (or at least turned in) draft.

What I call a **notes outline** may look like a half-page of brainstorming, but is far from it. Here a student ignores the introduction and conclusion (unless a really great idea comes along for it), for reasons that will become clear when I talk about the draft itself, and focuses on writing down and arranging the major points that need to be covered in the writing project. While the student may not have the points fleshed out, or may rely on prewriting for some of the details, he has something to work with that should fit the parameters of the assignment. The following is a notes outline for a movie review:

> Introduction with thesis
>
> what watching the movie was like
>
> how good the acting is
>
> problems with the story
>
> what I liked most about the movie
>
> my recommendation—conclusion

The disadvantage of a notes outline is that the writer may feel a bit up in the air about what to write. An advantage, however, is that that same up-in-the-air feeling may free the student to develop each idea in a number of ways. Points can be, in fact, developed more than one way and the writer later decides which one works best. It is also easier for the student to let go of a section that he is having trouble with to work on a different one or to let it go altogether once the idea proves to be going nowhere or poorly conceived.

A **chart** is a method of organizing and developing the parts of an essay so that 1) the writer matches supporting and developing material and 2) assures that all the parameters of a complex writing project (such as a research paper or a report) have been met.

The Value of Rest

I often suggest getting away from the computer (or desk if you write drafts by hand), and doing something that will take very little time (15–30 minutes) to give your body and mind a break from the rigors of writing. This should be done every hour or two, depending on your writing situation. Two of my favorite ways to "rest" are to wash dishes and walk. Washing dishes isn't really that exciting, but it has a definite beginning and end, and still has to be done. (Besides, the white noise of the dishwasher is oddly soothing.) Walking gets me moving around, giving me exercise I very much need, and this is actually good for writing. At home, I take one of my dogs out for a short "business" trip. At work, I have deliberately made sure my office is a good ten-minute walk from our division office, so that if I want coffee, I have to walk there to get some. Of course, doing so opens me to the risk of running into a colleague I might rather have a conversation with, but the risk is usually worth it.

The body can tire or get sore. The mind actually does need the body to help center it, even if the instincts are to keep writing for fear you will forget. If you have planned well, this won't happen, and my experience has been that when I write too long, the stuff I thought was brilliant as I drafted was mostly terrible after a good night's sleep had put things into perspective.

After neck surgery a few years ago, my doctor suggested (commanded really) that I get up out of my chair every 30–45 minutes and move around. That practice has proven invaluable to me, as I not only avoid the physical problems associated with my sedentary life, but also allow my brain to process what I have been doing and prepare for the next bit of work. It is amazing what a few moments of stretching or tidying up the desk can do.

Types of Drafts

Of course one can just sit at the computer and start typing. For most of us this only works when we have a great idea in our heads, fully formed, and are just so inspired we have trouble typing as fast as our thoughts. But that doesn't even happen to professional writers too often. Good prewriting and planning do help us in that regard but only take us so far.

Let me also state that for any type of writing, unless you know exactly what to say in the introduction and conclusion, you should consider waiting to write these parts of your essay until after you have drafted your body paragraphs. Many students give themselves writer's block right at the beginning by worrying about the introduction. Considering the purposes of the introduction and conclusion, you can see that writing these parts may be difficult until you know the body of your paper more.

It does help, however, to write the thesis statement before you compose your draft. This gives you something to think about as you write so you stay on track and reminds you of what your details should help to support. If you have a sentence you like for your introduction (not a re-working of your thesis), then write this, too. Compose the body paragraphs in the middle and treat the paper like a journey. Each paragraph between the introduction and the conclusion is a stop along the way between the beginning and the end.

If you are one to write a detailed outline, you probably have already decided an **outline draft** is going to work best for you. You essentially put into prose the thoughts and support you have already spent time organizing.

An outline draft has the advantages of providing the writer an easy-to-follow plan and giving the writer an organizational pattern to work with before committing a lot of time to writing. It also helps many writers to stay on track. Even if parts of the paper change dramatically, you are likely to have at least the basic parts you need and an organization you can feel comfortable with.

If you use a notes outline, then you can compose each section, which is likely to contain more than one paragraph, as you think of what to say. Here, you may skip around, focusing on the sections that you have the most to say about at the time you are working. (There is no rule that states each paragraph or section must be composed in the order in which it is read.) Writing this way can reduce some of the stress of writing by letting you focus on one section at a time instead of feeling like one part must be perfect before moving on to the next.

A **separate page draft** is one where the writer composes each paragraph (or each section of a longer essay) on a separate sheet of paper or in a different file. In college, before I had a computer to work on and at a point when I only had to type about one-tenth of my assignments, I often would work out my rough drafts by composing each section (sometimes each paragraph) on a separate piece of paper. Since then, I have found many advantages to this practice (even if I vary it by creating different files on the computer for each section).

First of all, it reduces stress by putting the focus on a small part of the paper instead of having to think of all the other parts that haven't been written. At the same time, I find that if I am stuck working on one section, I have less trouble moving to a different one and coming back to the "difficult" part later with fresh eyes. I can "experiment" with different introductions and conclusions, looking to see which one will be most effective for my audience and purpose.

Second, I feel much freer to work through my ideas and different ways to develop them. Sometimes I even write different things for the same section just to see what is going to work best. I feel more comfortable throwing things away or seeing if something I wrote for one section actually fits another section better.

Third, it forces me to develop my thoughts more thoroughly. If I write a topic sentence and maybe one sentence to go along with it, that puny paragraph looks as weak on the sheet of paper as it would be placed in the semi-finished essay. I am more likely to fill that page just so it doesn't look so empty if I need to. (Sometimes I find that the point I was trying to make in a section, having no support, is really support for another point in the paper. That works, too.)

A separate page draft also helps with organization. As we find that each section gets composed, we might decide that our original plan should include moving sections, or paragraphs within sections. As we will note in the section on revision, this can be a very important way to bring coherence to our writing.

In a **freewriting draft,** one writes using the prewriting notes and outline as a guide, but composes without regard to structure or coherence. Write everything that seems on topic, and use as many details and examples as you can, leaving the organization and "sense" to the revision process.

The advantage here is that you avoid that nagging little voice that tells you that something is not right or that a certain example isn't correct or that you need to make sure that you have spelled that word correctly before you move on. Many students hold themselves back from writing because they cannot silence that little guy. And when the paper is due, they usually revert to formulas, turn in a couple of painfully wrought paragraphs, or beg for an extension.

If you are the sort of person who sometimes has too many ideas and can't figure out what to write, as if there is a bottleneck at the brain keeping anything from coming out, then a freewriting draft might work for you.

Of course, there are serious disadvantages to this. One is that you will have to spend a great deal of time and work in revision. Sometimes a student writes a freewriting draft and figures that if the page length requirement has been met, then nothing more needs to be done. But with this sort of first draft, one is more likely to have written material off the subject or composed paragraphs in an order that will not make as much sense to the reader as it does to the writer. (Remember, what is clear in your head is not clear in mine.)

Expandable Paragraph Draft (The Mini-draft)

More than once, after a student has spent a good deal of mental energy on writing an essay, that student turns in something that amounts to a paragraph. Now, even the most understanding teacher is not likely to see that as a complete essay. Often this occurs because no prewriting has been done, so the writer has not done the work of thinking about what to write. But sometimes, after speaking with the student, I'll find that she or he really did agonize over what to say, often having done a good deal of prewriting (which sometimes produced even more words than the draft!). Sometimes the students want to just throw this away.

But wait! There's more.

Many times that seemingly puny little paragraph contains something to work with. Even if the sentences are little more than the notes outline put into prose form, those sentences contain the kernels one needs to build a good essay.

A **mini-draft** is usually just the general notes put into a short paragraph or two. This isn't really a draft, but it does help the writer to put ideas into topic sentences that usually sound better than the fragments and abbreviated thoughts one had before. The student can then take each major point or idea and create a single paragraph around it.

From here, the writer might be able to see, using her or his notes, what to add to each paragraph in order to develop them clearly. The writer can ask him/herself the following questions about each paragraph:

- How do I need to explain my point?
- What examples/illustrations would make the idea/point clearer or more vivid?
- Are there any words in the topic sentence that need to be defined?
- What details does the reader need to understand my point?

The writer can also follow one of the other forms of drafting to help expand her/his ideas. For instance, one could write the topic sentence on a separate sheet of paper and fill in the essay. (One can even go back to prewriting and do brainstorming or clustering on each individual idea.) The student can, using the single sentence, compose in a sort of freewriting fashion, and leave some of the hard stuff for revision. Or the student can make new, shorter outlines for each section and work from there.

Introductions and Conclusions

I advocate drafting body paragraphs before developing the introduction and conclusion for a number of reasons. First of all, they are very different sorts of paragraphs, and they need to be written and looked at differently. Second, often we don't know the best way to make an effective introductory paragraph until we "know" the body.

Sometimes, student writers feel that if they do not write the introduction first, they will not know what to say in the body of the paper. However, if one is planning the essay well, then the student can *begin* anywhere. There is no law that says each paragraph must be composed in the order it is going to be read. Further, much of writing is discovery. We often discover what we need to say along the way. No introduction is going to make that discovery for us, and if we fixate on the introduction, then we might lose the chance at that discovery.

An introduction serves two main purposes in your essay. The first is to give your reader an indication of where you are going. This is usually done via the thesis statement. The second purpose is to generate interest in what you have to say. I believe the second reason is more difficult for some students to grasp because they are used to writing for one audience, the teacher, who has to read the paper whether it is interesting or not.

The thesis statement is the guide to the paper. It tells your reader not only the subject of your essay, but the point you intend to make about that subject. Everything in the paper revolves around this statement, which is usually a sentence or two, and most often found at the end of the first paragraph. This is explained in greater detail in Chapter Three.

As you might have suspected after reading the sections of this book on purpose and audience, you should not assume that those who read your writing have to do so. Thus, it is vital that you work to gain their interest in what you have to say. They not only need to be drawn in but hooked. They need to have a reason, if only subconsciously, to continue past the first sentence.

There are a number of ways to get the interest of your reader.

- You can tell a brief story or anecdote that is pertinent to the main point you intend to make.
- You can ask a question that causes the reader to think about your topic or focus on the direction you intend to take your topic. (Be careful here though. Addressing the reader directly can sometimes lead to other problems, such as the overuse and misuse of second person.)

- Quote someone who knows something about your topic or give a piece of dialogue that gives the impression that your topic is woth being talked about.

Remember that you also have to make the connection between your thesis and your strategy of getting the reader's interest clear and smooth. It may well make sense to you when you write your first draft, but during revision, you will want to check that the introduction reads as naturally as possible.

One way to look at the introduction in your paper is to compare it to an introduction to another person. If you introduce two friends, you may just be acting politely. But you might expect the two friends to make a romantic connection. In that case, you would word that introduction in a way to perhaps make sure they were aware of certain desirable traits. However, if one of the friends worked as a manager in your company and the other friend was looking for a job, you would probably word that introduction quite differently.

You can think of your conclusion in much the same way. Just as an introduction gets people together, a conclusion is like the parting comments. But in your paper, you won't just say "Nice to have met you," and shake someone's hand. You want to leave a good impression because, like the introduction, it is the part of the essay that the reader is likely to most remember.

Some ideas for concluding your essays:

- Don't merely repeat the thesis statement. Particularly in short papers, it is an insult to your readers. It says, "You probably aren't smart enough to remember what I said to you ten minutes ago, so I'm going to tell you again." On the other hand, it is important to draw the main idea of the essay together or better help the reader to connect the body material to your main idea.
- If you used an anecdote in your introduction, make an interesting connection between the points in your paper and the story you referred to.
- Help your reader to see the ramifications or significance of your ideas without getting them started on a new topic.

Some don'ts about first drafts

- Don't take too long being "stuck." If, after fifteen to twenty minutes, you cannot think of what say, move on to another section and come back to the one you were stuck on later.
- Don't worry about getting every word perfect or about your grammar and mechanical problems. A good train of thought is often lost while fretting over where a comma goes. These sentence-level problems should be addressed in one of your revisions.
- Don't allow the first draft to be the only draft.

Revision

Revision is the most neglected (and perhaps the least understood) part of the writing process. It is also what can make or break your essay.

First of all, let's look at what revision **is not.** It is not editing or proofreading or running the spell check. These are essential parts of the process, but these come later. It is not "going over" the paper for typos or just to generally see how the paper "flows."

To *revise* a paper means to "re-see" it, to look at it with new and hopefully fresh eyes. First and foremost, it is to look at your writing as a reader would, not as a writer. And your goal is to improve what you have, not by fixing tiny mistakes, but by being willing to make wholesale changes—by adding, cutting, and rearranging significant material.

If we are to try and look at our writing as another person does, we have to know how people read. No matter how skilled a reader is, or what kind of reading she or he does, we all look for three things:

- Content—the general message of the writing and the development of that message.
- Organization—how the parts of that development are arranged to best illustrate and clarify the message.
- Sentence-level writing—includes not only the grammar and mechanics and punctuation of sentences, but also such elements as word choice, style, and tone.

Most of the time, we are not cognizant of these things as we read. We may notice these things more when they are missing or off kilter. For example, if a school teacher sends a note home with a child that the child was reprimanded for bad behavior, but does not tell the parents what that behavior was, then something is missing in the content. If you open a manual at work expecting to find the procedure for operating requesting supplies, but are just given a list of forms to fill out, then something may be missing in terms of organization. Should you receive an e-mail from your boss full of mistakes in spelling, typos, and emoticons, then you may find her or his directions very unclear, even if you can make out most of what she or he is trying to tell you.

And so it is important, as we look to make more than cosmetic changes to our writing, to try and think like a reader. We must try to imagine what someone who picks up our essays will go through as he or she reads it, someone who isn't giving a grade, but who perhaps doesn't even know this message or this information is useful to him or her.

Good revision may entail several drafts where significant changes take place. And it usually is most effective if the writer takes a top-down approach. That is, one should look at each revision or draft as having a different focus, starting with the biggest issues first. Also, each stage of revision may take more than one draft to complete.

In the first stage of revision, the writer should look at the paper as a whole, focusing on the message the essay is attempting to deliver and how well or thoroughly that message is developed for the reader. It is important to ask some questions of what you have and to be honest about the answers.

- Does the essay have a central point for a specific audience?
- Have you delivered what the thesis promises?
- What essential information is missing?
- What fits the main point but doesn't "contribute to the essay"?
- Is the essay organized so that it will best impact your readers?

Does the essay have a central point for a specific audience? Sometimes writers ramble about a general subject, not really getting to clear or specific point. Sometimes writers have more than one point and must decide which idea she or he most needs to develop.

Have you delivered what the thesis promises? Since the thesis is the central point and focus of your essay, you must make sure that each developing body paragraph points back to it and isn't merely about the subject. Sometimes we make associations or connections when we write a draft that make sense at the moment we are writing, but when looked at carefully don't really apply to the central message of the essay. Sometimes a writer will have a workable thesis, but all of the body paragraphs appear to point to a different idea.

What essential information is missing? It is common, particularly with first drafts, to put only the bare bones of the material in our essays, following an outline and getting the gist of development down. In our first stage of revision, we need to look at our main points and ask what needs to be illustrated or explained for our readers. Sometimes we need concrete details to help the reader "see" what we mean. Some points may need clear examples so the reader can mentally apply the idea. Sometimes we address concepts that are very clear to us but need to be explained in more detail to our readers. Remember, what is clear in your head as a writer may not be so for the reader.

What fits the main point but doesn't "contribute to the essay"? Another common problem with first drafts is that students, usually in an effort to fill the needed space, compose paragraphs that are about the general subject but do not really support or explain the thesis. The material may be merely a diversion the writer went on as he or she wrote. It may have been clearly connected in the mind of the writer at the moment of composition, but after some distance, looks only barely related. Maybe the writer needs to add a sentence to make the connections clear. Maybe the writer needs to cut the material altogether.

Is the essay organized so that it will best impact your readers? Students generally write the paragraphs of their first drafts in the order that those paragraphs came to mind. But that does not necessarily mean that the paragraphs should eventually be read in that order. We want our readers to follow along naturally so that each point follows the one before in a clear progression and isn't just a section to fill space. Sometimes we need to rearrange the body paragraphs so that the reader can move from initial interest to buying our argument. Sometimes we need to lead the reader from making a connection between something she or he knows is important to something you are trying to convince her or him is equally as important.

Note that at this stage, I am not looking so much at the introduction and conclusion of the paper. This is because these two paragraphs serve different functions and need to be handled separately.

After this stage, which may take more than one draft, comes the point where we look at individual paragraphs. Here, we are looking at the coherence of each paragraph and how well those pieces connect to the rest of the essay. Again, we ask some questions:

- Does each paragraph have one and only one central idea?
- Do all the sentences in the paragraph *support* that idea?
- What explanations, examples, and supporting details need to be either added or made more specific?

Does each paragraph have one and only one central idea? In some classes, you might have been told to wrap each paragraph around a **topic sentence,** a kind of thesis for the paragraph. This is not always feasible, but the concept is worth noting. Each body paragraph should cover only one element of your overall message. If you are the sort of writer who outlines thoroughly before writing, this probably won't be much of a problem. However, if you do not, then you have to test each paragraph. Sometimes students cover more than one idea in their initial drafts. Sometimes students write about the general subject but don't really have anything that develops the thesis.

Do all the sentences in the paragraph support that idea? Writers often think of things as they compose that sound good in their heads, but upon further inspection don't really address the main point of a paragraph. That might be a little diversion. It might be a sentence or two, perhaps an example, that does not clarify or explain the main point. Sometimes that sentence is necessary but should be placed elsewhere in the paper because it fits a different point. Sometimes the material needs to be cut altogether. It is possible that with some rewording the material can be re-shaped to fit the paragraph's central idea.

What explanations, examples, and supporting details need to be either added or made more specific? Most student writers write drafts that are merely the bare bones of what they need to say. Development is an essential part of a strong piece of writing. Often we need to explain our point for readers who are not familiar with our ideas. Usually strong, specific examples and concrete details give your reader a better sense of what you are writing about. They provide your readers with something to hang onto in their minds.

Here is also where some of the rhetorical strategies discussed in Chapter 5 come into play. You may need to describe an object in detail to help your readers "see" it. Your reader might benefit from a clear definition of a term, as you understand it. Comparing one situation with another the reader is more familiar with could shed some much needed light. Pay attention to your reader's need for clarity and vividness, and don't stray from your purpose.

It is at this stage where you might consider outlining your paper, especially if you are not prone to doing so during the invention phase of the writing process. As you note the arrangement and development of your paragraphs, an outline might provide you a strong visual of what needs to be changed to make each idea stronger.

As I mentioned before, introductions and conclusions need to be handled differently because they serve different purposes in an essay. Here are some questions you might ask of these sections:

- **Introduction**
  - Does it really give your reader an idea of where you are going?
  - Does it effectively get the reader interested?
- **Conclusion**
  - Does it give a real sense of finality?
  - Is it appropriate for your audience and purpose?
  - Do you end with a bang?

An introduction should, of course, contain a strong thesis, which is how you will tell your reader where the essay is headed. But sometimes a student writer starts in one direction and the rest of the essay goes in a different one. It is easier, for most, to revise the thesis to match the new direction than to change the whole paper to match the original thesis.

One should never assume the reader has to read your writing. Depending on your audience and purpose, you may need to try on different strategies for effectively getting that reader interested in your topic so that she or he will be willing to go past the first sentence.

Some students have been taught to repeat in the conclusion the main points of the essay. However, I believe this is a poor strategy for real writing as, in most cases, the reader can remember what those main points are, especially when the writing is fairly short. While you might need to give an overview of your ideas, typically that overview should be a single sentence, and certainly not the exact sentence you used as a thesis.

There are times when students end papers by delving into a new idea, one that almost seems to lead the reader into thinking that there is more to follow. Thus, the essay doesn't seem to really end. I have even noticed some students just stop writing once they reach the required word count. That reads like someone walking away before a conversation is complete.

It is also common in drafts to switch the purpose or forget the audience or purpose while putting together the concluding paragraph. For instance, a student might have the task of writing about a significant event, and instead of wrapping the paper up with an idea of what the event means to him, he tells the reader what sort of lesson she should get from the story. Or the writer might need to compare two products to determine which is a better buy, only to tell the reader something as generic as "Everybody has their own opinion, so it doesn't matter which you choose."

Your conclusion is the last impression you make with your reader, and as your introduction is the first impression, what you finish with is likely to stay with the reader, so try to end on a memorable note.

In the third stage of revision, you will work on sharpening your sentences and words. Here you will hopefully not only correct errors but make the sentences better for your reader.

- Read your paper aloud (or have it read to you).
- What sentences are not clear or logically put together?
- What words require explanation or substitution?
- Where have I been wordy or used vague terms rather than specific ones?
- What errors need to be fixed? Start with those you make most often.

Read your paper aloud. When we hear what we have written, we often catch those phrases that are awkwardly constructed or those misused verbs or other problems that make our prose less effective. Without knowing a great many rules about grammar or punctuation, we can often hear a sentence and just know it isn't right.

One way to approach reading aloud is to do it with a partner. Take a copy of your paper and give it to someone who sits across from you. Have this person read the paper as you follow along with a copy of your own. With a pencil in hand, stop the reader each time you come across a word or phrase that needs to be fixed until you get to the end. Sometimes it helps to start with the last paragraph and work your way backwards because, when we edit on our own, we often overlook what comes last, and for many people that is where most of their weak sentence-level writing occurs. Be sure to return the favor.

What sentences are not clear or logically put together? Sometimes when we write, a sentence makes sense in the first and even second draft. But when we isolate that sentence from the others, we realize that we might have started with one idea and ended with another, or that we repeated ourselves within the sentence, or that we threw in a phrase that makes sense to us, but is not going to make sense to our reader.

What words require explanation or substitution? We write about what we know, as much as we can, and sometimes we forget that we have experiences that our readers may not share. So if we use words that will not be clear to a reader, we should probably explain them. This isn't limited to words that only we know. For instance, when I worked in a grocery store, one of my daily tasks was to *front* the store. The word *front* is one that many people know, but the meaning they assign to that word is probably different from the one I came to learn. At the grocery store, the word meant to pull items to the front of the shelf, thus making the shelf look full. If I wrote about my experience sacking groceries, I might need to explain that word.

Sometimes we also need to change words that we have used, possibly because we have used the same word several times or because we used a word that is not likely to communicate clearly. I once had a student who, in writing about his car, used the word *car* more than twenty times on a single page. He could have used other words for car to avoid repetitiveness. He also could have combined some of his short sentences to liven up his essay and keep it from sounding choppy.

Some students even use words they do not know because the words "sound good" or seem to come from a big vocabulary. Yet such misuse of language is likely to cause you more trouble as your reader will not likely know what you mean. If your reader is your teacher, then you may only show the opposite of what you intended: that you are a smart person with a good command of the language.

A word of warning here: A thesaurus can be a useful, but also dangerous, tool. While helping you, one hopes, to find the right word for the job, some students use the thesaurus merely to help them come up with words they believe mean the same thing. Some students try to use it like a dictionary that will help them find bigger, more impressive words. Don't use a thesaurus without using a dictionary as well. You should understand every word you write, especially if you expect your reader to understand them as well.

Where have I been wordy or used vague words rather than specific ones? It should be the goal of every student writer to learn to use words as precisely and deliberately as possible. Because students worry about making sure a paper reaches a certain length, they sometimes write long, winding sentences that do not communicate as clearly as they should.

Also, we may be used to using certain words to describe our experiences because those we talk to can either read our nonverbal cues or know what we mean when we use those words. But without precise language, communication gets stalled, and sometimes the reader gets confused. For example, once a student wrote in an essay that seeing her father at her graduation made her "happy." Later in the essay we find that she had not seen her father in years and she is jumping up and down for joy. Because the word she used at first was so vague, what followed was not so clear.

At the same time, we must be careful that we use words we understand well. I have had many a student misuse a thesaurus or just toss words into a sentence because they "sounded smart," when the word only made them look silly.

A word about peer review. You may have been in an English class before where the teacher had students bring rough drafts to share with a group. Students divided amongst themselves, read through the essays quickly, and made a couple of proofreading notes. Typically, each member of the group was told by the others that her or his paper was "really good "or "just fine." Sometimes students turn in rough drafts to a teacher, who marks them up expecting them to be returned corrected.

Unfortunately, these are inactive and ineffective methods for writing. Having someone tell you how wonderful your essay is without giving you real feedback on how to improve only serves to reinforce poor writing habits and give students a false impression of a writer's abilities and areas that need improvement. Even when the teacher marks errors, the student rarely learns much and usually makes the same mistakes each time he or she writes. Little is done to improve the content or organization of such essays.

Thus, it is important to revise with specific goals in mind, and the same goes for peer review. Preferably that review will also take a top down approach, where the bigger elements of writing are handled first and the sentence-level problems addressed last. You can use the questions provided to help not only with your own efforts at revision but also to help when working in groups. The best environment will also include questions that are directly related to the assignment, as this is where many students miss the mark in their papers. If you have someone else help you with an essay, someone you trust or a tutor in a writing center, then you should have a copy of the assignment handy in order to help that person help you most effectively.

Other Ideas for Improving Your Writing

Learn from your mistakes and from your success. Most students never read what their teachers write back to them, and most are not even aware that a teacher may spend twenty-thirty minutes grading and marking a single essay. While I do address this in another chapter, it is important to look at any feedback you have been given on an essay, even if you are satisfied with the grade. Some of that feedback might be about what you did well, and you certainly want to keep that up.

Develop a positive attitude about writing. I am aware that this is easier said than done, particularly for students who have struggled with writing or who have had some negative experiences involving writing assignments. However, instead of looking at each assignment as a barrier, try seeing it as an avenue to learn or to express something important, and you might be surprised what kind of energy you can bring to the project. Instead of worrying about how a paper might expose your flaws to others, try to see yourself getting conditioned for writing in the same way a personal trainer helps you reach your fitness goals.

Work on finding connections. It is easy to see each writing assignment as a self-contained task that bears no connection to the other parts of your education, or even to other parts of your English course. However, we all need to keep our brains working and making connections. Try to look at what your writing has to do with what you read for your classes. How do the concepts you have applied to the essay relate to concepts you learn in other classes? How can improving your writing help you to make better grades in classes that involve fewer, but higher percentage, writing assignments? The more connections you make, the more you are likely to see what is valuable in your overall education, and the more likely you are to find some enjoyment in assignments that once were drudgery.

Chapter 5

DEVELOPMENT STRATEGIES

Writers use a number of rhetorical strategies, or modes, to develop their ideas. Which developmental mode you use at what point in your writing is largely up to you, but you should always take into account your audience and your purpose. Of course, the instructions of your professor have a great deal to do with that in college. One should read the directions of each assignment carefully. Rarely in real writing will one mode be all that is used. Most likely, you will employ one mode in a section or paragraph while using another somewhere else in the same piece of writing. You may even need to experiment as you draft to see which works best.

Narration/Description

Telling stories is as natural to human experience as falling in love or arguing with siblings or laughing at a joke. If we look back at our day, we may find that we have told little stories all along the way: answering a question about how our weekend was, telling what it was like shopping for a new car, or explaining why you were late to class. And while there are some who seem to be natural storytellers, we need to know that we can learn to write a good narrative when called upon to do so.

When might you be asked to write a narrative outside an English class assignment? You could be asked in a chemistry class to tell about an experiment, from start to finish, in a report for your teacher. You may, on a history exam, be required to recount a significant event before explaining how it shaped a law or led someone to an important decision. In a psychology class, you could be asked to provide a "day in the life" of someone with a mental disorder or learning disability. On the job, you could be asked to write an Incident Report, detailing what happened when someone got injured. If you are a supervisor, you could be asked to write about your observations of employees for their performance reviews.

If asked by your English professor to write a narrative or to include a narrative in your essay, you will more than likely need to narrow to a specific moment or event that you can detail and elaborate upon. For example, a narrative about your senior year of high school or the entire nine months of your pregnancy would take a book to adequately detail. However, an essay can easily house the story of your prom or the moment you first held your child. While the amount of time is smaller, because the focus is narrower, the writer has more space for showing what is important and more latitude in how to shape the details.

Good stories revolve around the central events or key moments. In fiction or movies, they are sometimes referred to as plot points. This is the general outline of *what happened*. It might help to list these points in a general outline before writing about them. This way you can eliminate those that are not really important to the story or combine those points that seem to go together.

The narrative should revolve around a culminating event, a moment where the story hits its peak and from which all the details should point.

Also helpful is to know why you are telling this story. Are you trying to connect the event to a decision in your life? Are you using the story to illustrate a point? Are you trying merely to entertain your audience? No matter how serious or frivolous your story, whether you are talking about the best concert you have been to or about a near-death experience, the purpose should drive your choice of details and the effect you hope your story will have on your audience.

If you listen to good storytellers, you will notice that what usually sets them apart from others telling the same story are tone and description. An active writer will not merely report events, but construct a compelling narrative where tone is controlled and deliberate. Tone is the mood one conveys in a story. You cannot assume that the reader will, for instance, look at the story with a very serious attitude just because you believe the subject matter is serious. You need to be aware of the adjectives you use and the balance of short and long sentences to convey the mood you want your reader to have.

In addition, it is imperative to use specific and concrete description in your narrative. Description is more than telling the reader what something looks like or sounds like. It is about appealing to all of the senses, but also about appealing to the reader's sense of things. Good description also helps the reader to "see" and "hear" (and taste and smell and feel) in their minds more of what has happened. These are also called sensory details.

As you compose or revise your story, you may need to identify the most significant people, objects, and moments. This will give an idea of what needs specific description and what can be left alone. You also need to look at the dominant impression you want your reader to have about those details. For example, let's say you are telling the story of a date that went badly. You might then focus on what the date chose to wear in contrast with your attire. What was it like riding in the car on the way? If the person driving had high expectations, you could describe how immaculate the inside of the car was and the serious tone in his or her voice. On the other hand, you could show that a date was not good because of how little care a person took with his car.

Descriptive details should be as specific and precise as possible. Not only will precise pictures help your reader to visualize and hear the events in their minds, it will help them to be clear about your intent and about the events themselves. For example, while the words *mad* and *upset* may seem to say the same thing, they may not convey exactly what you want. Once, I had a student who described himself as "a little upset" by something a person had told him. In the next paragraph, the writer had punched that person in the face. My first reaction upon reading this was to think, what psychological problem does my student have that he goes from "a little upset" to throwing fists so quickly? When the student and I discussed his essay, he revealed that he was much angrier than his words let on. So we explored ways he could explain and demonstrate that anger. He substituted the word "seethed" into his narrative and added details such as clenching and unclenching his fists to his description of the moment and suddenly the punch made a lot of sense.

Compare/Contrast

Simply put, to compare two or more things is to focus on significant similarities between those things. To contrast is to look at significant differences. One need not do both in a single paper, but it may be useful to do one or the other as a method of development.

Comparison is one of the most natural modes of thought we can engage in. For instance, unless we know exactly what sort of car we want to buy and have the means to obtain it, we are likely to make comparisons between several models or perhaps the same model sold at different dealerships. One car may get better gas mileage; another may make us feel good to drive; another car may cost us less in insurance or in maintenance later "down the road." Since not all of our most important criterion may be available in the same car, we have to make choices about what we buy based upon our needs and our desires.

For example, while I may prefer a small car that gets good gas mileage and might be easier to insure, I may need something larger for my family. Here I am also looking at the significant differences between vehicles. If I have to buy a van for my family, then I would not compare it so much to a Jaguar or a Volkswagen.

I might even list what qualities I need in a van and then look at the differences in those qualities. As a father, I need to be mindful of safety and how much the van would cost me up front as well as later in gas and maintenance. I might want to weigh different sizes, based on the sizes of my children. If my children are small, one minivan might be appropriate for my needs over another that would be better for teenagers.

Do I want (or can I afford) the extras that can come with a minivan, such as television and DVD player, or special air conditioning features? Are there hybrid models available, and, if so, what are the benefits of driving a hybrid over a standard minivan?

You should be able to see two things here. First, much in the way of comparison and contrast, as a mode of development, concerns qualities and values that you, as a writer, may need to define or explain for your readers. You don't want to assume that everyone has the same values. Second, you need to focus on what is significant. Making observations about what is obvious or not very important only serves to fill up space with empty words. That is, your comparisons and contrasts must serve a purpose.

Process

When you write about a process, you either demonstrate to your readers how to do something or how something is done. The first mode is often referred to as a "how-to." We might call the second "how-it's-done."

In an essay, you might need to give your readers instructions on how to do accomplish something. A how-to essay (or essay section) will contain the following:

- easy to follow directions
- explanations, where necessary, of what the reader is doing or why the reader is doing it
- warnings—notes to tell the reader when the process is not going correctly
- encouragements—notes to tell the reader when the process is going well
- results of the doing the process

A how-it's-done essay (or essay section) sometimes will include steps, but if so, will usually have fewer in favor of expanded details about each step. For example, in a political science class, you might be asked to explain how the Electoral College works. Rather than give all sorts of sub-steps and warnings or encouragements, your instructor may want to you spend more space explaining these steps. If the essay is for an exam, you may only need to explain what those steps are. On the other hand, the teacher may want you to analyze one of these sections in detail.

If you were writing a report for a chemistry class, you may need to explain the process for an experiment, but also explain the ramifications of using different chemicals or different amounts of the same chemical at a particular stage. The point is you are not likely, in real writing, to write a paper using just process. It may form the bulk of the assignment, but not the whole thing, so it is important to see how this mode works with others.

Examples/Illustrations

Somewhere in your essay you are making a point or, possibly, several points. To help your reader to understand that point or to "see" it the way you do, you can use pertinent examples to illustrate what you mean. For instance, let's say you are writing an essay where you explain how you enjoy books more than the films made from them. You could easily list the reasons this is true for you. However, your point will be made clearer if you give examples of books and movies you have experienced, describing in detail what made the reading experience more enjoyable for you.

You might notice that examples often take on the characteristics of other rhetorical modes. For example, if you wanted to make a point about how you cannot enjoy a horror movie, no matter how hard you try, you could tell a couple of stories with specific details about when you have watched different horror films.

Cause and Effect

When we look at the *cause* of something, we try to determine what brought that event about. When we look at *effect,* we mean what happened as a result of something. Both modes are useful in developing certain kinds of points or ideas.

For instance, in a political science class, we might need to explore how and why voting patterns have changed at different times in history or in a particular area of the country. We might try to make an argument demonstrating the causes for voter apathy or look for the reasons why an area that traditionally voted for candidates in one party suddenly switched to another. In a course on substance abuse, one might need to trace the various causes of addiction in order to understand various methods of treatment. For a speech class, you might try to persuade your classmates that changing the school's tobacco policy has helped the overall health of students on campus.

On the other hand, when looking at the effects of one thing on another, we may need to trace events in the opposite direction. For example, in a history class, you might be asked to explain the economic and political effects of the abolishment of slavery after the Civil War. For a social work course, you might look at the various effects of poverty to understand why teenagers drop out of school. For a nutrition course, you could look at how certain foods raise or lower cholesterol levels.

When using either of these modes of development, be careful that you do not confuse cause and effect. Understand that unless you can trace a clear line between one event and another, you will have difficulty communicating any connections you are trying to make. And notice that when you look at a trail of events, you are likely to see a multiplicity of factors.

For example, let's say that you are trying to explain how someone who made mediocre to bad grades his first semester now makes good grades. One could make a fairly reasonable assumption that the person had decided in college to study more. But that answer is too vague and does not take into account what changes he made and why, in an environment where most find good grades even harder to achieve, that "extra study" paid off in better grades.

So you might look at what the student means by "study," and you find that the student does read from his assigned textbooks every day. He had read before, but usually after the material was covered in class, and just prior to exams. Further examination reveals that he also takes lots of notes and rarely misses class, whereas before he skipped several class meetings, and when he came he was often sleepy due to a heavy work and party schedule. He still works and goes out with friends.

So what makes him more "present" in class? What changed that has him reading before class instead of cramming at the last minute? What had happened that his efforts now have greater rewards?

Digging deeper we may find that he could not change his work schedule, so he changed his class schedule. Instead of classes that begin at 8:00 a.m., he starts at 10:00 a.m. We find that while he does have an active social life, he reserves drinking for the weekends. We wonder what made him change his habits and find out that after an accident near the end of the previous semester, his parents warned him that if he didn't make better grades they would no longer provide the money he needed for school.

Classification/Division/Definition

To classify something is to put it into a category your reader can understand or needs to understand. Division is the mode where you distinguish things in one group from another. Definition is where you explain what something means.

We frequently put things into categories or groups, often without realizing it or knowing why. We have friends and acquaintances, for example. We might even further categorize those people based on any number of criteria, such as work friends or drinking buddies. These distinctions help us to describe our relationships with other people. We also place things we regularly experience, such as television shows or music, into categories.

Some categories seem ready made for us, but we may find it necessary to make finer distinctions within categories. For example, most people are familiar with the terms Republican and Democrat as the names of the two predominant political parties in the United States. We tend to think of politicians in these broad categories as having the same philosophies, and yet this is not true. You may have heard terms such as "fiscal conservative" to describe someone in the Democratic Party or "social liberal" to describe a certain Republican. You may have even become familiar with those who describe themselves as Moderates.

Even within genres of music, we have what some might think of as subcategories. For instance, within the general description of jazz, one finds big band jazz, bebop, "straight ahead" jazz, West Coast jazz, fusion, avant-garde jazz, and "smooth" jazz (which some fans say isn't real jazz). Each of these categories has its own unique characteristics.

When writing about classifications and divisions within groups, you have to note the distinguishing characteristics. In some cases, this might be as simple as pointing out what can be readily observed, such as the differences between a "muscle car" and the average automobile. In other cases, this may be difficult because even those who regularly discuss the subject may not agree on the characteristics or which characteristics deserve the most emphasis, as in the case of varieties of some genres of music.

Argument/Persuasion

In Chapter Six, I deal much more specifically with argument. However, you may find that for a paragraph or two in other papers, you will need to use some of the characteristics of argument and persuasion to develop your thesis.

With persuasion, you are trying to get your readers to take your side. Argument may seem to be the same, but it is slightly different. Argument is the attempt to show that a point you are making is reasonable. With argument, you may not need to get your reader to take a particular action or think a particular way, but you are hoping that the reader will willingly give your idea a fair and reasonable chance.

With either argument or persuasion, you need two main elements: 1) a position you take on an arguable topic and 2) support for that position. Support is essentially the various reasons you take for that position. One should not make assertions and expect the reader to accept them without a rationale.

In argument papers, the writer must take a great deal into account that we need not address here. However, if argument is part of your writing project, suffice it to say that clear and logical connections must be made between your assertions and your reasons for believing them.

CHAPTER 6

ARGUMENT

For many students, the word *argument* conjures up thoughts of ugly and mean-spirited confrontations, where there is a lot of yelling and not a lot of listening. Perhaps they think of what happens on talk shows or a recent fight they had with their parents or significant other. These are anything but pleasant, and since they usually bare no fruit, the association leads some to believe that argument is useless, at best, as an intellectual exercise.

Some students see argument as an interesting challenge, and these students often believe they are good at it, though many are not. They get a rush while arguing, as one might in the midst of a battle they feel sure they will win. Perhaps the student has a strong vocabulary or prides herself on being able to think quickly on her feet. Maybe the student has been able to quickly see the flaws in an idea and is able to dismantle his opponents' positions. Often students believe they are right about an argument merely on the strength of their feeling. That is, if one *feels* deeply or passionately enough, the student may think that the argument is already won.

However, in the academic world and, to a large extent the real world, argument should not be seen as a conflict or a competition. Surely, there are different sides that seem in opposition to each other, and perhaps one may see the goal of an argument to win others to one's side. But looking at argument in this singular way is likely to bear little actual fruit.

When we see argument merely as a conflict we must overcome or a competition to be won, we often lose our understanding of the purpose of the argument or the audience we are presenting that argument to. For example, if a teenager asks a parent to use the family car for the evening, and the parent says no, the teen may ask why not but not be willing to listen to the reasons. He or she may further exacerbate the situation by calling the parent names or by shouting about the parent being unfair. The teen forgets that the person who is able to grant permission is not likely to respond well to name calling, perhaps because the goal suddenly turns from getting use of the car to vindicating oneself.

Part of the problem is that most have a limited view of what argument is. We should not always see argument in terms of conflict and competition. This is not to say that an argument is not, to some extent, about conflict or that competition has no place in rhetoric. However, what typically occurs is a scenario where real discourse and intelligence is missing, replaced by merely the adamant and ill-thought-out quarrel. Hence, most people see argument this way:

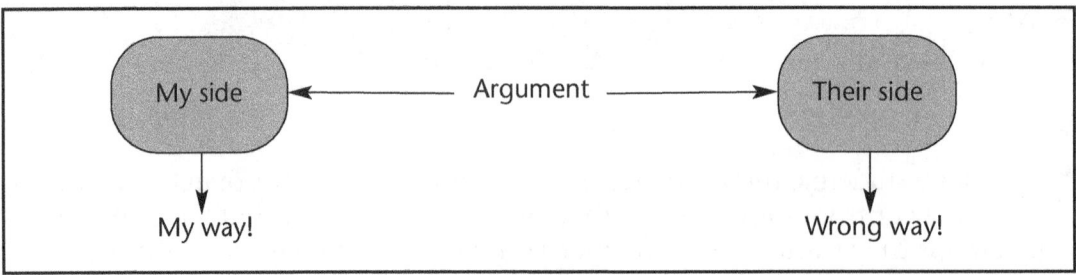

Here the goal of the argument is not to attain the truth or even to express what one sees as the truth, but merely to be *right*. Consider for a moment how this might be true. I have known a number of people who will realize during the course of an argument that they are completely wrong. That is, they become convinced that their own position is not right or at least that they need to reconsider that position. Yet, these people will refuse to let on that they have come to this realization, instead continuing to argue their original point. Now they are taking a stance for something they no longer believe in!

Why? Because many people are more concerned with *proving* themselves right than in actually *being* right. This is, I believe, a mistaken notion of what argument is all about.

Take a moment to think about a group of people you have had a number of arguments with. For many, your parents are the ones with whom you most often voice disagreements. Now, take a few minutes to consider recent arguments you have had with that person or persons. Then get out some paper and list all the reasons you lost those arguments. By lost, I mean you did not get your way even though you believed you were right.

After you look at your list, you will likely find that in many cases the reasons for not getting your way had nothing to do with you being right or even persuasive. And whether one gets one's "way" matters as much in *how* one argues as in how right or justified that person is.

Consider the arguments that take place over a subject that is familiar to many students (even us older ones)—the curfew. A close look at the typical argument over such matters tells us a great deal about the wrong way to approach the subject of argument.

When does the argument over curfew take place usually? Well, it actually takes place in different forms at different times, but the main argument takes place just when the teenager is heading out the door for the date or time with friends. The other time this takes place is when the teenager gets home, usually late (if the young person arrives on time, then there is nothing to fight about). In the first place, the exact time the teenager is expected to return home may not be set as a general rule by the parents. That is, they may be flexible to some extent, allowing for age and particular circumstances. In the latter case, there is usually some sort of family rule that is assumed to be understood by all parties.

Whether the teenager is going in or coming out, the argument ensues, and it is rarely a calm, rational discussion. Why not? Because there are bigger issues for both sides as to why this conflict exists and how it can and should be resolved. Further, because each party has a vested, *emotional* interest in the outcome, it is difficult to act fully in a reasonable manner. And one person acting reasonable does not insure that the others will.

What are the issues for each side? For the parents, there are the issues or concerns of trust, authority, and loyalty. They want the teenager to trust their experience and judgment. They want their authority as leaders of the household to be recognized and respected. They want their child (and no matter how "adult" one feels, you are still a child to some degree to your parents) to be loyal to the rules and ideals that are part of the family.

What does the teenager usually want, other than just to be able to stay out and have fun with her or his friends? She wants to be trusted. She wants her parents to recognize that she is not a small child that needs constant protection and that she is smart enough to avoid bad situations, and if not smart enough to avoid them, at least smart enough to deal with them. The young person wants to be respected as an adult, one who hopefully has earned the right to prove himself responsible because he has previously proven himself responsible. He wants to be treated differently. If he has a younger sibling, he may want rules to be amended to reflect the fact that he is different from that sibling.

So what should we look at when we think about academic arguments? First of all, we should see our goal as showing to reasonable people that our position is indeed reasonable. This is one, perhaps subtle, difference between argument and persuasion. In persuasion, we may not be dealing with reasonable people, or at least people who are open to our position, and so we must take measures to influence the readers or listeners to get to that point where they are open.

Second, we should see argument as something that people do, not only naturally, but in order to grow and adapt to various situations. Deciding between two similar products to purchase is a kind of argument. We may need to weigh a number of factors before making a purchase, and even if the choice does not work out, we can learn from the results and incorporate them into the next decision process. In relationships, we do not always come to definitive conclusions where one person wins over another, and often it takes the argument in order for important facts to come to light and even for us to learn about ourselves.

The Basics Parts of an Argument

All arguments contain three basic parts: the question, the thesis (answer), and the support. While many of these parts of the argument may not appear clearly or obviously, our understanding of the argument may depend largely on how well we understand the role each of these parts plays.

The *question*. Every argument revolves around some subject or some issue. But the question we are trying to resolve about that topic is usually not asked directly. Nonetheless, this question, and how we ask it, is as important as our answer.

When we write arguments, our question needs to be specific and concrete. It also needs to be answerable. We should have more to work with than something that is easily answered with a "yes" or "no" or "agree" or "disagree." Most real issues are more complex. In addition, our questions should not imply a ready-made or obvious answer.

For example, let us say we are interested in improving the parking situation at our school. We should not ask "Do you think that the school should build another parking lot?" or "Do you agree the parking problem is bad?" Such questions are vague and tell us what we want the reader to think. We haven't clearly stated what the "parking situation" is. Is it a problem of finding a space during peak hours of the day? Is the parking lot unsafe, either for cars or the people driving them?

If our question revolves around solving a problem, we have to clearly understand what that problem is. We don't start with the proposed solution. Perhaps we can ask, "What can students do to insure they can park close enough to get to class on time?" or "What can the school administration (or campus police) do to reduce the number of cars being vandalized or broken into?" Perhaps the problem concerns a specific, but temporary, situation. "How has the construction work that has closed one large parking lot affected students who use the daycare facilities?" or "Has the school lost students due to potholes and other hazards in the parking lot?" might be questions worth asking here.

Note that in many conflicts people are asking different questions and sometimes do not realize it. For instance, if my wife asks me what I want for dinner, but really wants to know what I am willing to cook, she is likely to get an answer that does not satisfy her. Asking yourself why you didn't do your homework is not the same as asking what distracted you or what you can do to avoid distractions.

Remember that when reading arguments the question is usually not asked directly. You must read carefully, usually working backwards from the support and thesis, to determine what that question is. But misunderstanding that question usually means misunderstanding the whole argument, and that is likely to spell trouble.

The *thesis* is essentially our answer to the question. It is the main point a writer attempts to make in an argument. Note also that the thesis needs to be specific, clear, and supportable. Qualifying a thesis statement with phrases like "In my opinion" does not usually help, because if arguments are only about opinions, then we are still hoping to get the reader to side with that opinion, or we are writing about some topic where the reader can do what she or he wants no matter what.

If we look at the questions we asked previously, we can see that they have several possible answers, and, in some cases, there is not necessarily a single "right" answer. And if we wish to make a strong answer, we must recognize that few answers are simple or obvious. If the answer is simple or obvious, we have no need to write in defense of it. To the question of what students can do to insure they get a closer parking spot, we might easily say, "Students should leave earlier so there are more close spaces to choose from when they get to campus." On the surface this is probably a true statement. However, it does not take into account that leaving earlier is "vague" or that even if we understand what the phrase means, leaving earlier may not be possible for all students. Some students could leave five or ten minutes earlier but not an hour sooner than the time they usually do. Some might even say that they have tried leaving earlier only to find themselves with more time to find the same far off parking spot.

We could qualify the statement to say that *some* students could try leaving an hour earlier than usual. That is better, but not much to write a paper around. After explaining how one would do this and the possible benefits, there is not much else to say. Perhaps in this situation, the writer could posit a number of possible solutions—such as carpooling, riding the bus, or creative scheduling of classes—and thus reach more people with a variety of possibilities.

Our thesis statement is not a subject and not a question. It is the specific answer to the question. It must leave room for clear support. Again, if the thesis is obvious to our readers, we have no need to write about it.

Many students believe that an argument stands on its thesis, but that is only partially true. Without a strong, clear thesis, the argument goes nowhere in several directions. However, the strength of an argument is in its *support*. These are the reasons we have for the answer we have given.

Support is built through a variety of means. Most simply, we give our reasons for the position we are taking, but if we want the argument to be effective, we need to do more than list those reasons. We certainly need to explain those reasons, make clear connections between those reasons and our thesis, and probably illustrate any claims or sub-points we make.

We must provide evidence for our claims. Merely repeating them or demonstrating how strongly we feel will not suffice. Some of that evidence may take the form of data or facts clearly connected to our claims. Some may take the form of syllogistic reasoning. We also support our points with carefully written counter-arguments and concessions.

Verifiable facts. Here we provide information to our reader that helps us to see a point in its clear light. If we look at our argument concerning parking lots, for instance, we can give data about what times of the day the lots are the most full and connect that information to the times when most students are on campus. That would support the point that while there may be a sufficient number of spaces, those that provide easiest access to the building are nearly always full during the hours most have classes. We could also demonstrate that some students have breaks between courses during which they could move their vehicles closer. Or the writer could show that while some students take the same classes as their friends, they often come in separate vehicles, and thus support the suggestion of carpooling. We might even do research to show how much money is saved by the average student who rides a bus to school.

Expert testimony. It certainly helps an argument to have someone on your side. But that someone does not have to merely give an opinion that mimics yours. Those who have specialized knowledge—often because of their education, training, jobs, or life experiences—can give us information or a perspective that cannot be easily seen by the average person. In our parking lot scenario, we might talk to a school administrator about the cost of providing a shuttle bus service or the chief of campus police to determine how often students are ticketed for illegal parking. An engineer or architect might be able to help the writer see how difficult it would be to build a covered area where students could gather to wait for a shuttle bus.

Syllogisms are pieces of reasoning where the writer supports a conclusion with clearly connected premises. The most common example is the following:

> All men are mortal. (Premise 1)
> Socrates is a man. (Premise 2)
> Therefore, Socrates is mortal. (Conclusion)

For the reasoning to be valid, the premises have to be true and properly connected to each other. If, for example, Socrates was a fish or an idea, and not a man, then the premises would not prove the conclusion (even though fish are also mortal as far as we know).

We use this sort of reasoning often without realizing it, and if we read carefully, we can see the same sort of reasoning in the arguments we read. In fact, it is vital for us to be able to identify these parts when reading in order to construct good arguments, whether we are making use of or refuting what we have read.

In order to construct solid arguments, we must anticipate and/or acknowledge any possible opposition to our thesis. Inactive writers ignore their opposition, usually worrying that bringing it up will damage or contradict their main idea, but this is a big mistake. You are better off acknowledging the point that would attempt to bring your argument down, fairly and honestly, and then raising a *counterargument* to that point. For instance, one might point out that starting a shuttle service would be too costly. The writer could refute this statement by stating that after the initial investment of one or two vans and spaces for pickup, the campus would be able to maintain the vehicles in house with the crew already tasked to take care of such things. Further, the writer could note that the service would only need to be run during peak hours of the day and could be "on call" for other times, such as in poor weather or for poorly lit areas of the campus. The vans themselves might contain advertising that might offset some of the costs.

Concessions occur when we look at a point our opposition has made (or might make) and explain why we agree with that point. To concede a point is not to concede an argument. But it is usually wise to show where you have common ground with your opponents. It may be that both sides have the same goal in mind but a different way of approaching that goal. For our argument over the parking lot, we might have to concede, for instance, that not every student would be in a situation where carpooling is possible or there might be barriers to a shuttle service other than costs (such as licensing of drivers).

Two philosophers have had a significant impact on how we look at argument. Carl Rogers suggests that effective argument takes the time to focus on the common ground between opposing sides. Doing so allows the writer to bridge gaps between those sides by appealing to what is best for all. It also forces the writer to adjust the tone and language to be more accommodating. Stephen Toulmin reminds us that arguments often carry what he called *warrants,* or underlying assumptions, that may need to be acknowledged or addressed. Some of these warrants may well be connected to the goal or purpose of the argument. For example, one might say that it is an assumption that improving the parking situation is better than leaving things as they are and forcing students to adapt.

Appeals

Another usually unstated portion of each good argument is the use of appeals. A writer appeals to the reader in three main ways.

Logical appeal. The logical appeal is not where you tell the reader that your argument is "common sense" or "perfectly clear." If your point was common sense, then there would be no need to write about it. The logical appeal is how you demonstrate to your reader that you have based your conclusions on sound reasoning. This means that your paper will have a notable lack of logical fallacies, or errors in reasoning. The essay will follow a natural progression where the evidence clearly (to the reader and not just you) supports your thesis.

Ethical appeal. The ethical appeal is where you demonstrate that you, as a writer and thinker, have been fair and honest about the topic and all evidence. Merely telling your reader you can be believed will not do. It is like telling someone you are humble. You have to demonstrate that you have fairly represented opposing positions and have weighed all sides carefully before reaching a conclusion.

Emotional appeal. One might think that the emotional appeal is where the writer tugs at the heartstrings of the reader and uses lots of exclamation marks to show how strongly the writer feels about the subject. However, the emotional appeal is not about showing how you feel, but demonstrating to readers that they should take an interest in the topic and in your ideas about that topic. Instead of thinking in terms of topics everyone has a strong opinion about (such as abortion, war, or the death penalty), consider those times when you thought something was important that those around you did not care about.

Logical Fallacies

Logical fallacies are errors in reasoning that occur when one misuses, misunderstands, or just plain misses evidence. One can think of the acronym STAR when testing the evidence in one's own argument or analyzing the arguments one reads. Evidence supporting an argument must be *sufficient.* That is, there must be enough of it to reasonably support a point. Evidence also must be *typical.* The examples or data that you use to develop an idea should not be outside what is normal for the situation or topic. Also, any information you provide the reader must be *accurate* and accurately applied to the claim it is supposed to illustrate. Last, all evidence must be *relevant* for the situation and the conclusions you have drawn. You will find that examples of logical fallacies fail in one or more of these tests.

The following is by no means an exhaustive list of logical fallacies but those I have found to be most commonly used in student writing. Remember, your goal is to avoid these in your own arguments.

Attacking the person (sometimes called the *ad hominem* argument). This fallacy occurs when the writer has ignored the opponent's argument and ideas altogether and, instead, turned the focus on something related to the person or character making the argument. Politicians use this frequently, calling an opponent some name or focusing on an element of the opponent's personal life that has nothing to do with the specific issue she or he has been called upon to address.

A writer has used a *hasty generalization* when he or she has based a claim on too little evidence or evidence that is not typical. You should avoid grand statements like "Nobody is doing anything" or "Everyone wants to ___." For example, if you go into a store and you see only one person who is not helpful, it would not be reasonable to say that people in this store do not care about their customers. A single person rarely can represent the whole company. Further, if you came at an unusually busy time of the year (say the Christmas holidays) and the person helping was not personable, it would not be fair to say that all the employees are distracted and rude.

The *bandwagon* fallacy is sometimes referred to as an *ad populum* argument. (*Ad populum* is Latin for "appeal to the people.") Here the writer or speaker tries to get the reader to go along with an idea on the sole basis of its popularity or wide acceptance. It is the same argument teenagers use sometimes when they try to convince parents to allow them to do something because "everyone" is going to do it or "all" their friends will be there.

An *appeal to tradition* is similar to the bandwagon fallacy in that the writer suggests that because something should always be done or approached in the same way it has been for a long time. An example of this is the argument that a girl should not be allowed on the high school football team because football has been a man's sport throughout history.

An *appeal to pity or fear* is an attempt by the reader to feel sorry or afraid about a situation and thus ignore points that do not favor the writer. An example of this is when someone who wants to see less restrictions on gun ownership states, "If we limit the number of guns a person can have, then you will get robbed or your wife will get raped." Of course, it is important for a writer to demonstrate that her or his ideas should receive attention, but when examples are not logically connected to the claim or cannot be proven or verified, then the writer has made an error.

Begging the question is sometimes called *circular reasoning* because the argument goes in circles. Instead of supporting a point with specific information or reasoning, the writer repeats the claim in different words. "The teacher should not penalize me for plagiarizing my paper with a zero, because then I would get a bad grade in the class," is an example of this sort of thinking. The bad grade *is* the penalty. Here the writer is trying to deflect attention from not abiding by the rules by focusing attention on how the penalty will harm him. Another example might be to say, "Teachers should give extra credit, because some students don't do all the assignments." By definition, *extra* credit assignments are in addition to what was already required, not *instead of.*

When a writer deliberately uses a word that can mean different things to different people or in different contexts, and so attempts to manipulate a premise, that writer is guilty of *equivocation*. For instance, if a politician states that a vote for him is a vote for freedom, he is expecting you to believe that if elected he will safeguard those freedoms that you hold dear, even if he has not specifically mentioned what they are. Further, he implies that his opponent does not wish to protect those same freedoms. Another example is where a writer uses a word that may be emotionally charged, even though its actual meaning may vary from context to context, such as in labeling an image as pornographic. The writer may believe that any image of nudity (even Michaelangelo's David) or reference to sex (such as "The Song of Solomon" in the Christian Bible) is pornographic, even though by legal definition it is not. The reader has to be careful not to be swayed by the use of a word with negative connotations.

When one distorts the words that someone else writes or says so that a new meaning exists—one not intended by the original speaker—then that person is guilty of taking something *out of context*. Consider the following example: A woman running for a position on the school board states, "We need to quit rewarding poor teachers with raises." Her opponent states, "She is against pay raises for teachers." The second candidate has misrepresented his opponent in a way that is likely to make her appear to have ideas that she does not have.

A *slippery slope* argument is one in which the writer assumes that a single event or action will necessarily bring about a chain of events that will end disastrously. For instance, one might claim that watching a particular television program will cause teenagers to act wildly in imitation of the show's principal characters. Years ago, a popular advertisement for a particular oil filter had a mechanic telling viewers, "You can pay me now or pay me later." The implication was that if people did not buy that particular oil filter, something terrible would happen to the engines of their cars, thus causing them to incur great expense. The fact that one could avoid the problems by purchasing another oil filter or selling the vehicle was, of course, ignored.

The *false cause* fallacy seems to work in the opposite direction of the slippery slope argument. Here one assumes that one event was necessarily and only caused by an event that preceded it. The Latin phrase *post hoc ergo prompter hoc,* which means "after this, therefore because of this," is often applied to such reasoning. One common example is when someone goes out to eat at a restaurant and later gets sick. The person then blames the restaurant for the illness. A number of factors during the meal could have made the person ill (poorly cooked meat, badly washed dishes). However, the person also may have done other things to cause his problem, such as drinking copious amounts of alcohol during the meal or contracting a flu bug (which can be in a person for some time before manifesting itself in nausea).

Analogies can be useful in argument. They can help a writer to explain a complex idea by comparing it to something easy for readers to understand or relate to. However, the writer must be careful not to commit the *false analogy* fallacy. This happens when the writer compares two things that only have a few elements or points in common. For instance, stating "He will be a good teacher because he is a good student," is not reasonable. A good student and a good teacher may share certain characteristics, such as knowledge about and devotion to a subject. One might even argue that both have to communicate their ideas about that subject clearly. However a significant difference is that the student communicates knowledge in the form of tests and essays read by the teacher. A teacher typically communicates that knowledge via lectures, demonstrations, and activities for a broader and less-informed group of people.

The *false authority* fallacy occurs when a writer refers to someone who appears to know something about a subject when the person has no real expertise or experience concerning the matter. Advertisers routinely use famous people to supposedly illustrate the value or superiority of a product, for example.

The *either/or fallacy* is also known as the *false dilemma.* In this case, the writer has presented only two options or solutions when many may exist. For example, one might argue that one can either support a particular spending bill or have the elderly living without health care. Usually the side the writer opposes is presented as "obviously" absurd, so that the only alternative appears to be the side the writer champions. Often, the writer presents a great deal of specific information and data in support of her position, and only mentions the opposing side in a cursory and superficial fashion.

The *red herring* argument is also known as a *fallacy of distraction.* One might try to derail an argument about one topic by mentioning different issues that also could be important to the same audience. For instance, the writer may ask, "Why should we worry about safety in parking lots when the cost of tuition and books continues to rise?" Here the writer minimizes the importance of one subject by drawing attention to another.

The phrase *non sequitur* is Latin for "it does not follow." This fallacy is also known as the *irrelevant argument.* Our earlier example where a teacher and a student are compared might be an example of such reasoning. One might say that a person being a good student does not tell us anything about how well that person will perform as a teacher (or any job for that matter).

Logical fallacies work on readers (and listeners) because they *appear* to make sense on the surface. Often, that is because the reader wants something to be true when it is not. I have noticed that some students will say that a piece of reasoning is full of fallacies (which they usually cannot identify) when they disagree with the thesis. Other students will fail to see fallacies in an argument whose conclusions they believe are true. This is why you must read carefully both the arguments you come across and the ones you write. While many fallacies are deliberately rendered, some come from ignorance. But no matter how they find their way into a piece of writing, they do hurt the credibility of the writer.

A few last words about argument:

- Argument does not need to be flippant or vicious.
- Argument is not an intellectual exercise.
- Good arguments do not employ deception.
- Good arguments are about persuading reasonable people that your position is reasonable.

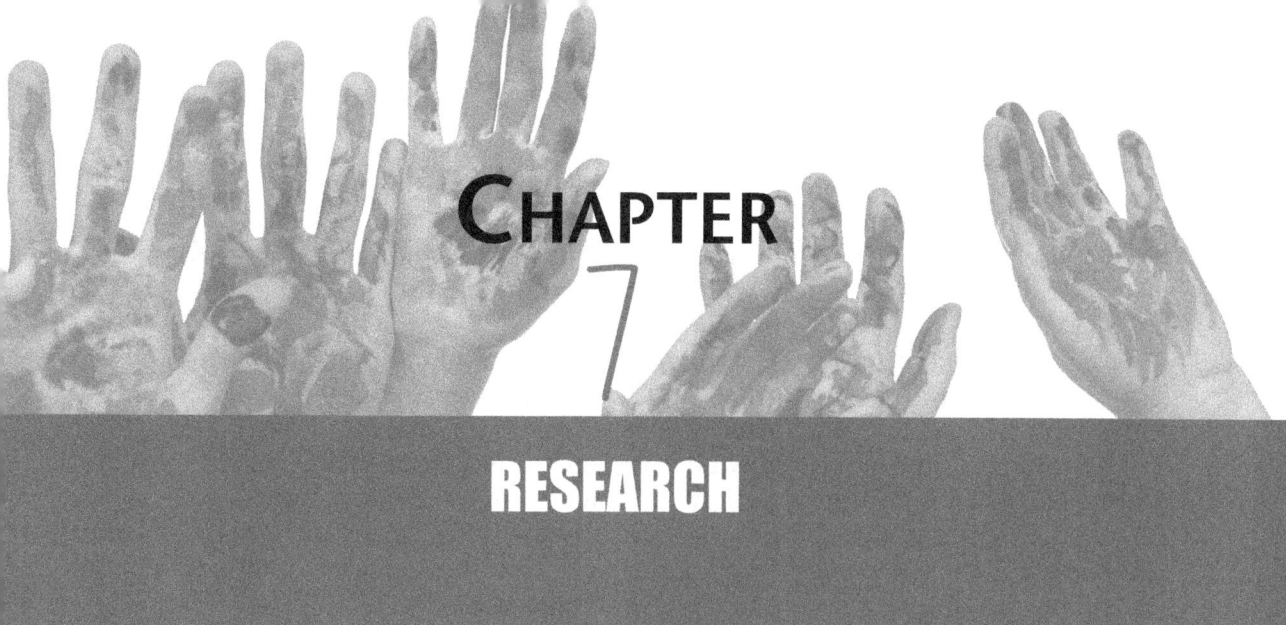

Chapter 7

RESEARCH

*E*ven students who can appreciate the fact that writing will be in their professional future have a hard time seeing the value of doing research papers. After all, how many jobs actually require workers to analyze *Hamlet* while seeing what several other people say about it? Of course, such an approach does oversimplify, and even trivialize, the subject. But the question remains: Why is learning to do research and then incorporating that research into writing important?

Much of what a student does in college is predicated on research. Not all of that research is of the variety that requires reading copious documents and books. One might be expected to find differing opinions on a court case for a political science course. You could be asked to research case studies for a psychology course. Perhaps you will be asked to repeat experiments for a chemistry class that had been previously done by famous scientists.

In addition, while compiling the opinions of a handful of Shakespearean scholars is not what most people are going to be doing after college, you might be surprised at where you will find a need to do research and write about the results. For example, your boss might ask you to write a report after looking into different companies who produce software your company is considering for purchase. You may need to write about the options available for the use of a building for your club or church. In order to write a strong letter to your congressman, you might want to find out about what she or he has voted for and what her or his rationale was for those votes.

What makes research so difficult? Anything that we don't want to do becomes tough to do right away. Further, doing research can seem overwhelming, even for rather short projects, because there seems to be so many parts to the process that are difficult to manage at once. Research papers are also different from other types of writing that we can sometimes put off until the last minute or that fit neatly into formulas we can remember.

To help us past the difficulty of writing useful research, we do need to understand what research is for and what research is not.

Research is not finding five guys who agree with us. Our job in doing a research paper is not to come with a fully formed opinion and then search out a certain number of sources who will confirm that opinion. Sometimes we are asked to research a topic we don't have much knowledge of, and thus we must inform our opinions before we develop responses to them. While research papers would be easier if we just quoted a handful of people who already saw things as we did, we need more than those quotes to make a solid argument. We need actual information and data, as well as developed reasoning. We also need to demonstrate we have looked at other possibilities or ideas.

Research is not the compilation of data. We are not to merely cut and paste a lot of information about a topic and tack on an introduction and conclusion. While there may be assignments in college where we are asked to put together a good deal of information, we still have to do some critical thinking on our own. We may not need to come to any conclusions about the information, but we may be expected to connect that information with a specific idea or concept.

Research is not a task we only do for sadistic college teachers. Research is actually an outgrowth of trying to reach our goals, even if we don't always do as much work looking for the right car for our family as we might writing a research paper over a character in *Hamlet*. Unless we have all the money we need, and we know exactly what sort of car we want, we will do well to do a little research on the sort of vehicle that best fits the needs of our family and our budget. Sometimes we find we have to do research projects as part of our work. In fact, it is good to do research in order to find a job in the first place. Further, our lives are not just made up of what we do at work and for school. You might be surprised at how much research can improve some of the other elements of our day-to-day lives.

Procrastination is a serious enemy of research projects. Despite the claim that some students make that they "write best under pressure," waiting too long to do research puts more stress on the student and often causes greater problems down the road. One of the excuses some students make for plagiarizing essays is that they "ran out of time." Usually the student has merely not spent the time well and finds him or herself in a difficult situation when the paper is coming due.

Procrastination also limits the student's choices and the time it takes to make choices. Look at this first from a merely practical point of view. If you are required to use book sources for your paper and you wait too long, many of the best sources are not likely to be available as they were at the beginning. Even if you can do your work with electronic sources, which presumably do not run out, you still have less time to weigh which sources are going to work best for your paper. Many students just find what they can and try to force-feed material into a paper that cannot easily accept it, creating a hodgepodge of quotes and statements that lack coherency and provide weak arguments. Procrastination also gives your writing little or none of the momentum sorely needed for a long and complex project. Road blocks are inevitable. Life sometimes gets in the way. But the sooner you start, the easier it is to crash through those roadblocks when necessary or to alter your course.

Before any research project, it is important to plan your attack. Often, students take an assignment and just run with it, heading to the library or the search engine with a general topic and hoping that they can find something worthwhile. This problem is made worse when the student is not sure what she or he is going to write about. Thus, you should consider a few things before wandering about and wasting time and energy.

Understand the parameters of the project. Some of this is about how many and what kind of sources you need, how many pages your paper should be, and what documentation style is expected. But those are minor compared to what you are expected to find out and what you are supposed to do with the information you gather. Develop a research question that helps to guide your search for information and ideas. This way you do not research a general topic but focus your search on what matters for your topic. Don't worry if you do not have an answer to your question at first. That is why you are doing research.

You may find it helpful to see how the project you are working on fits with the rest of the course you are taking. Often, suggestions for research have been included in your reading assignments. Sometimes an instructor wants each person in the class to research a different topic with the goal of educating the whole class, so that as a whole each project serves to give more concrete material to apply to the theories and ideas discussed. Sometimes a research project is meant to serve as a mini-proposal that a student can modify later for professional purposes.

In developing your research question, you need to *think about what you know and don't know about your topic.* Are assumptions and preconceived notions the basis of what you "know" about the topic? What do you need to find out about your topic to better understand it or to weigh various theories? What makes the topic important for others to be informed about?

Consider making and sticking to a schedule. Some classes will impose a research schedule on you. But in many others, you will be given the general guidelines for a project at some point and the only other thing you will have is a due date. It will be up to you to spread the process out so that it is easily manageable. Try to make reasonable time for coming up with a topic, researching your topic, and writing and revising your paper. Even if something comes up to put you off the schedule, having something planned will make it much easier for you to adjust and get back on track.

Ask questions in a timely fashion. "What are we supposed to do?" is not a good question, particularly when the due date is only a couple of days away. Do your best to understand your assignment and to write down questions when you are confused. Try to make those questions as specific as possible. You may want a detailed outline of what to do, so all you have to do is plug in your research, but most assignments do not work this way because you are expected to think and discover a great deal on your own. However, if you are confused about something as you go along, you need to get that problem clarified right away. Putting it off only makes it worse.

For example, I sometimes limit students in their research parameters by restricting the use of .com sources, though I do expect them to find some of their sources electronically. For a student who is used to finding all their information via Google, this requirement may be confusing. But unless asked to clarify this specific part, the student might not learn that they can use the library's online databases or education (.edu) or government websites (.gov).

Some Ideas for Gathering Information

Find three to five times the number of sources your instructor requires. For instance, if your teacher wants you to have two outside sources, try to gather six to ten. What many students do is make a brief search in a library catalog or search engine and then take the first two or so items that appear. Later, when writing the paper, the student gets into trouble because there isn't much in those sources that is useful, and she or he has no time to find anything else. Finding more material means you have more choices to make, and you can use the best sources for your paper instead of the first ones that appeared.

One does not have to read all of these sources word for word. As you will see later in this chapter, you can employ some strategies to determine which sources might work best without spending a great deal of time with them.

Understand the value of timely sources. Some facts are always facts and always will be. However, most topics have undergone an evolution of sorts, and out-of-date material is likely to hurt your argument because it shows you have not really looked at the topic carefully or considered all the information available.

Use your research to develop your thesis and come up with ideas. While it is great when circumstances in writing a paper are such that we have a fully formed argument in mind before doing research, and all we have to do is plug in the material where it is needed, most often we have only a general idea of where we want to go with a research paper. Plan to read and write at the same time, so you can discover a specific point of view you can develop clearly and carefully.

Don't forget the other side. In most arguments, there are not just two sides, but many. And as we learned in the chapter on argument, it is important to acknowledge those sides, if only to counter them or to concede where parts of a position are shared. Remember also that while you may not have the same opinion as someone else, there are reasons why those opposing positions exist. It is important to get at the heart of these positions in order to develop clear and fair arguments.

As you get used to the research process, you need to *develop discernment so that you can determine which sources are most credible.* One might easily dismiss what one disagrees with and too easily embrace what one already agrees with. But remember that arguments stand and fall not on their conclusions, but on their support. It may be that in your opposition there is a kernel of truth or a point well worth considering. And someone on your own side may have a flaw in his or her reasoning that needs to be addressed.

Remember also that bias is neither bad nor good. It just is. But we have to be able to see when bias has gotten in the way of good reasoning or when it has marred or skewed the facts, even if that bias is on our side.

Where your instructor will permit it, do not be afraid to use an unusual source now and then. Most students limit themselves to the books and articles they can find via a traditional search. However, sometimes it may be useful to watch a documentary film, conduct a survey, or interview a subject matter expert. These sources may be outside the parameters of the assignment (and thus "extra" research), but they can bring life and immediacy to the paper that makes it more interesting and thoughtful.

How Can You Tell If a Source Might Be Useful?

If you are doing research well, you will come up with three mental piles of sources. You will run into articles and books that will have nothing, it seems, to do with your topic, are outdated, or provide nothing more than what you already know. These go into the "No" pile. You will probably run into a couple of sources right away that you will say "Yes" to. These will include data and information that you can see immediately will be useful in your paper, even if you don't know where.

The biggest pile is likely to be the "Maybe" pile. These sources might contain useful information or ideas, but you won't know for sure until you have had a chance to read them more carefully and thoroughly. Since at this point of the process, you are not reading everything you find word for word, you set this aside as a possibility.

The truth is that with good research it is difficult to see what is going to be useful or valuable until one begins to flesh out an outline for a paper or begins to draft that essay. Even after a rough draft is written, we might realize a source we didn't use at first might be just what we need. This is one reason I strongly advise doing more research at the beginning than you need and keeping track of that research with a working bibliography.

A **working bibliography** is a list of all the potential sources for your paper. It should contain everything from the "Yes" and "Maybe" piles, and may even grow after you begin to write your draft. There are a number of advantages to using a working bibliography other than having at hand those sources you were not sure about at the beginning. Another advantage is the ability to keep sources together when it is time to construct the Works Cited page. If you list sources in proper MLA style, then you need only copy information for those you use. Also, a working bibliography can be helpful for future research. One never really knows when a topic will come up again, and a source that is not used in one paper may well be perfect for another.

As you do research, you should keep in mind at first that you are trying to merely gather potential sources. You are going to take more time to read and consider what you find after you have brought them together.

Look at the table of contents and index of books you are considering. You may quickly see that a chapter of the book corresponds directly to the topic you are writing about or that one of the subjects is addressed in a couple of pages in the book. This way you can go directly to the material you are interested in without having to read the entire book to find it. You might also notice that, for many libraries, the table of contents or general subject matter is listed with the online catalog. Thus, you might not even have to physically see the book before you rule it out or decide to list it on your working bibliography.

When using online databases, articles often come with an **abstract***, which is a short summary of the article's contents and conclusions.* You can read this summary, most often only a couple of sentences, and easily determine if the article is potentially useful. Never quote an abstract in your paper, as it isn't really the article. If you decide to use an article, you will have much more specific material to work from.

You should, when possible, test the credibility of your potential sources. While it may be easier to find something you want on Wikipedia or About.com or Yahoo Answers, these are not reliable sources and should not be included at any time. Sources for which bias will clearly overshadow the content should be omitted as well, even if you have a philosophical agreement with the group.

Consider that some sources should automatically carry more weight in terms of credibility than others. For instance, since anyone with access to a computer can create and post to a blog, these pieces are not, in general, as thoroughly thought out and researched as something posted on a university website and written by a scholar in that particular field. Postings in a discussion board forum are typically hastily written and often take the tone "I'm right and anyone who disagrees with me is an idiot," which should tell the discerning student that it isn't likely to be useful for college-level research.

Along with credibility, students should be careful about the timeliness of each potential source. Since with many contemporary topics, what we know and what is prevailing in research can change rapidly, having sources where information is missing or out of date hurts your credibility as a researcher, so much that is not current should probably be discarded.

Of course, timeliness, like credibility, can be a rather elastic concept. One cannot set a clear cut-off date for all subjects. For instance, research into a classic work of art or literature might not need strict time parameters, while research into something like childhood obesity or bipolar disorders would. When in doubt, consult your professor's preferences.

Checking Reliability/Credibility

The average student writer does not have at her or his disposal all the tools or resources or time that might be needed to fully investigate every potential source. However, there are questions one might ask about sources that one is unsure about.

Note that with major publications, such as a large newspaper or trade magazine, a process is usually in place that attempts to insure honesty and fairness. Fact checkers, editors, and proofreaders are often employed to authenticate and confirm material, sometimes even for opinion pieces. Even though a publication or publisher may lean in a particular philosophical or political direction, it is in their best interests to at least give the impression of fairness and honesty.

You must also be able to tell the difference between fact and opinion when you read, a skill that is not as easy as it may appear on the surface. I have had several students who, given different articles, could not spot those where an opinion was being argued (as in an editorial or blog) or tell that a strict news item (containing little more than dates and places and names) was not offering an opinion.

What are the author's credentials, expertise, or background? While in mainstream articles this is difficult to determine since most are written by professional writers who are researching and reporting on a given topic, in many cases we can see that the writer is someone who has particular knowledge of a subject that most of us do not have. Perhaps the writer is an expert in the particular field the article or book is about. This is usually the case with articles in scholarly (often called peer-edited) journals. The writer might also have been an average citizen with a unique perspective. For example, a mother who has gone through the experience of trying to get a teenage drug addict clean might be able to offer insight into the process that someone pontificating from the sidelines cannot provide.

Of course "experts" also have their biases. They do not know everything, and it helps when a writer is able to be honest about his limitations. It is also incumbent on the student researcher to read well enough to see where bias has gotten in the way of full disclosure.

What in the work (article/book/webpage) shows that the writer knows what she is talking about and has been fair to all sides? Just tossing out a handful of unsupported assertions or unverifiable statistics does not mean that the writer has done her homework. Has the writer presented information that shows more than one perspective? Does the data seem to support one position without giving space to an opposing position? Is there a fair and reasonable counterargument? Are there concessions? Does the article contain any logical fallacies?

Further, tone and language can tell the researcher a great deal about whether a writer is likely to have been honest and fair in his or her reporting and writing. If the writer takes a particularly emotional tone (usually eliciting anger or pity), then that writer likely may not have looked at the topic with an unbiased eye (and probably does not want you to either). If the writer uses name calling (*ad hominem*) attacks or superlatives to describe people, ideas, or even facts, then you have reason to doubt the fairness of what you are reading.

Is there any documentation provided? In peer-reviewed journals, articles typically end with some sort of bibliography, and we have the opportunity to check the sources. But even in articles published in mainstream newspapers and magazines, writers give us a hint as to where they received their information. They refer to interviews they have conducted and other books and articles they have read that contained information pertinent to their topics. The absence of such references does not mean that a piece of writing is flawed or inaccurate, but the more information a researcher is given, the more one should want to know where it came from.

What do you know about the publishing organization, company, or website? Publishers, like any other business, want to make money. The desire to run a profitable business does not mean that a publisher does not have integrity. However, if the publisher or company has an obvious philosophical or political bias, it should be noted. That bias does not automatically mean that anything the organization prints or posts on the web is to be ignored, but we should be aware that the bias may get in the way of us gathering all our facts through them.

If you go to a website for a product, you are not likely to see much information about the problems with the product or articles explaining why the product is no good. On the other hand, you may still find useful information about that product.

Writing the Research Paper

Once you have gathered your sources or potential sources, you need to get started on the writing process. Even if you are mostly planning and organizing your ideas, you should not wait to write, as you are likely to lose momentum. Remember that getting started early also helps us through difficulties that may arise.

Have a working thesis. Even if you change this later, it is better for you to have a goal to write towards than to just meander through your topic, hoping for a point to emerge somewhere. Remember your goal is not to merely fill a certain number of pages but to make a point you expect your research and reasoning to develop. Make that thesis as specific and arguable as possible, hopefully answering your main research question. Remember it may change or be modified later.

Plan. As noted in Chapter Four, everyone plans his or her writing differently. Some like to construct detailed outlines, while others prefer to write a bit freer and need only a general plan of organization to get started. Either way, it is important to take the time to figure out what your main point is and as many of your supporting ideas as you can before you write. You may have drafted rough paragraphs as you have done your research. This is good, but be sure to incorporate these into the general sketch you are putting together.

To keep from being overwhelmed by the immensity of a large project, try to look at your research paper as a series of short essays that are linked together. Just as a short paper is a series of paragraphs put together into a coherent whole, your research paper is going to contain parts that may require a good deal of space or very little. For example:

1. Introduction and statement of thesis
2. Background Information
3. Supporting Point #1
4. Supporting Point #2
5. Supporting Point #3
6. Concessions
7. Counterargument
8. Importance of topic
9. Conclusion

This outline is, of course, rather general, and no section would receive the same amount of space or information. The introduction would likely be only a single paragraph, while any of the supporting points may require several pages because it would contain the bulk of the research and analysis necessary to support your thesis. One might find after beginning to draft that one does not need to devote an entire section to the importance of the topic but can incorporate ideas from this part into the conclusion and/or introduction. A writer may well find more than three supporting points. The bottom line is that a plan will help you to compose each part without the interference of the others.

One of the values of a good working plan for writing is that *if you become blocked as you write one section, you can always move on to another* and come back to the difficult section later. Sometimes as we write, we realize that we may need a bit more research to flesh out a particular idea or that we just cannot find the right example to illustrate a point. Don't worry. You can go to a different section, work on that, and come back later.

Make sure the focus and thesis are applicable to the assignment. I don't know how many times I have seen a student do a good deal of interesting research and solid writing only to find out that parts of the paper (sometimes the whole thing!) are inappropriate for the parameters of the assignment. You can help yourself by reviewing your assignment before planning and perhaps incorporating important elements into the plan itself to keep you on track.

Do not let the research do the writing for you. As noted before, research papers are not cut and paste jobs. Depending on the parameters of your assignment and your goals as a writer, you will need to flesh out points with your own critical thinking, analysis, and ideas, making connections between some points and explaining some others. The paper should have your voice and your stamp on it.

Write about each main point, and then stop. Understand the value of rest. Starting early and making a good plan will give you this advantage. Some students, riding an adrenaline high or afraid they will forget something, try to write the bulk of their research papers all at one sitting. They fool themselves into believing that what they have written after sitting for an hour at the computer is the best stuff they have ever come up with, but after looking at that material later, they find it is usually the weakest. It is good to save the file and get away from it for awhile to give your eyes and mind a rest before tackling the next section. But don't worry. Your good plan will help you pick up where you left off with relative ease.

No padding. Padding is the addition of unnecessary material to an essay, usually in order to reach a certain requirement in length. Sometimes it takes the form of long paragraphs on related, but superfluous, material. Sometimes a student adds quotes here and there to short paragraphs, quotes that have no clear connection to the material around it. Sometimes the student just adds several sentences of "BS," hoping that the instructor will just gloss over that material in his haste to get it graded.

But this material almost always detracts from the goal of the writing. It takes the reader away from the central point and may well confuse or annoy that reader. If you write a draft and find that it has not met your instructor's length requirements, consider that something is likely missing from your paper in terms of developing or clarifying your points, not just mere words to fill up space.

Consider writing your introduction last. While I said previously that it is best to start with a working thesis, some goal toward which your paper can work, it is important to note that the thesis is only part of that introduction. Another important role of the introduction is to get your reader interested in what you have to say, and sometimes it is hard to know the best way to do this until the body paragraphs have been drafted. So, avoid generic openings or rambling about the general subject until an idea hits you.

Keep in mind as you write your draft that you will revise. If you find that a particular section is not working for you or if material does not seem to be coming together as clearly or coherently as you know it should, do not despair. Hopefully, you have time to revise and make the paper stronger. Unless you are waiting until the night before an essay is due, it is okay to let go of the first draft for a short time.

Revising the Research Paper

In addition to what I have discussed in the chapter on revision, I have a few suggestions for improving the draft you have written.

Consider outlining your paper. After writing the draft, make a very detailed outline of the points and support in your paper. This should give you a visual idea of where your argument needs more concrete material, such as research or stronger reasoning. You should be able to see if there are paragraphs that have gone off the topic or that need to be re-shaped to fit the thesis. You might even have to revise the thesis to fit the body of the paper. You might even find that you need to move parts of the paper around to better impact your readers or to make ideas clearer.

Double-check that all the parameters of the assignment have been met. This can be done by checking some of those parameters against the post-draft outline. But it is good to read through the essay carefully and make sure that nothing has been included that should not have been and that everything required (number and types of sources) has played a significant role in the essay.

Check your transitions. Since I suggested that you divide each part of the research paper into smaller, connected papers, you will need to help your reader get from one section to the next with clear transitional sentences or words. If one section does not naturally fall after another, consider moving it so that each part will make better sense for your reader.

Account for all sources and double-check all documentation. For every reference you make in your paper to outside sources, you must have a corresponding Works Cited page entry. For every Works Cited page entry, you must have at least one reference in your paper. Check both ways and make certain both your internal documentation and Works Cited page follow the proper MLA guidelines.

Check your sentence-level writing. After all the work you have put into the paper so far, you do not want grammar and punctuation errors to hurt your effort. Take the time to do more than "go over" your paper. Proofread and edit the essay carefully, sharpening sentences, eliminating wordiness, and strengthening word choices.

Get a helpful opinion. With as much work as a research paper can be, one can easily lose sight of flaws that another set of eyes can provide. Therefore, it is usually to your advantage to seek help, even if you believe yourself to be a strong writer. But you do not want a mere proofreader.

Whether you have a friend who is a good writer or use the services of a writing center tutor, you should take your assignment with you. This gives your reader a chance to see what has been required and what you needed to avoid. Thus, that reader can give you an idea if all the requirements have been met from the perspective of someone reading, not one invested in the composition of the paper. All revision should have a goal that is more specific that "to make it sound good" or "see if it flows."

You should get more out of writing a research paper than a headache and a grade. Many students may not see the value of putting this much work into a research project because they know that the teacher is not likely to see all that work. In college, the professor is often not grading the process, but the final product. However, just as on the job when one prepares well, adjusts to difficulty, and revises carefully, and that effort (we hope) is clear to the boss, so the difficult and sometimes arduous process described here should pay positive benefits.

Chapter 8

DOCUMENTATION

Documentation is one of the most-often neglected and least understood elements of writing. Rather than go into the reasons for this neglect, I would like you to consider the following scenarios.

Scenario One. You notice that a particular task that must be done every day at work takes twelve steps according to the manual. However, the task often is fraught with problems and the output is not always what is desired, so the task has to be repeated, which wastes valuable time and resources. You have figured out a way to get the same job done with seven steps. You've tested it out and found that not only does the job get done faster, but with fewer mistakes, thus avoiding repeated work.

You bring this new procedure up to your boss and he tells you it sounds like a good idea. "Write it up," he says enthusiastically, "and put it on my desk." For the next couple of nights, you spend your own time writing and drafting and revising your idea, and by the end of the week have a tidy little proposal on his desk.

A couple weeks go by where you wonder what has happened to your proposal. You are about to ask your boss about it when, during a staff meeting, your boss' boss hands out a small packet outlining your suggestion. Your boss' name is the only one on the proposal you see in front of you, and he is getting hearty handshakes from everyone for innovations you came up with.

Scenario Two. What if you were pretty sure that you needed to fire someone but were worried that this person might cause a fuss or sue the company? You would need to document the problems that lead to dismissing the employee and have that information easy to read and find in case you had to have it in court. One could not rely on hearsay or rumors about a person's negligence. You might need copies of time cards to show a pattern of being late, e-mails to demonstrate inappropriate behavior, and performance reviews to prove a pattern of shoddy work.

While to the average student documenting sources often seems like an unnecessary pain, it is a vital part of any writing involving research. Not only does it serve to demonstrate that you have done your due diligence in finding good material for your paper, demonstrating much of the work you have put into the project, but it also acts as an essential element of your argument. You give your readers a way to check your sources, so that your points carry the greater weight of having been vetted. Using a clear and standard documentation style, you also show respect for your reader because you avoid any suggestion you have something to hide.

There are several documentation styles, but the two most used in college are from the Modern Language Association (MLA) and American Psychological Association (APA). In this book, I only cover MLA documentation because it is the style used in English courses and the Humanities.

MLA documentation is divided into two distinct, but connected, parts: in-text citations and the Works Cited page.

In-text documentation is also called internal documentation or parenthetical documentation. These are the citations one puts in the essay itself, usually at the end of a sentence when research has been referenced. *Internal documentation* is sometimes called parenthetical documentation because the material you provide your reader is placed in parentheses. Internal documentation is quite easy to understand and to apply. Basically, it entails placing a page number or an author's last name and a page number in parentheses after quoting or paraphrasing material from your source. Here, you must know whether you are quoting a text directly or paraphrasing. Either way, you must show where you got the information.

If you take material from your source and copy it word-for-word into your paper, the quoted material **must** be placed in quote marks (""). After the quotation, you place your parentheses for internal documentation.

> Neil Postman writes, "the form in which ideas are expressed affects what those ideas will be" (31).

or

> One critic of popular media states, "the form in which ideas are expressed affects what those ideas will be" (Postman 31).

Note that the first example only includes the page number where the quote is found in the parentheses while the second uses the last name of the author and the page number. The name of the author is not necessary in the first example because it is included in the text of the paper. However, because we do not have it in context in the second example, it is necessary. Note also that the period in both cases comes after the citation.

Another form of quoting is important to note here. This is the **block quote.** The block quote is used whenever you need to reproduce a large amount of material from your source. The general rule of thumb is that you do not use the block quote unless the material will cover four full lines of text in your paper (or is four or more lines of poetry). The quoted text is then set off from the paragraph by indenting it ten spaces (two tab stops). No quotation marks are used and the page number reference will come after the period. Also, keep in mind that the quote is still double-spaced.

According to Michael Schumacher:

> Carver's survival is testament to the resilience of the human and creative spirits. His second collection of stories, *What We Talk About When We Talk About Love* . . . was a sort of catharsis, a compilation of works stylistically stripped to the bone, an anthology of the pain and despair his life had become. (216)

Try to keep your block quotes to a minimum. If you have several in a short paper, you give your reader the impression that you have done very little thinking or writing of your own.

Sometimes you will not quote material directly but put it in your own words. This is particularly useful when you have quite a bit of text that you can put into a shorter form or when the material needs to be put in language your reader can better understand. The rules for internal documentation are the same with **paraphrasing** as they are when quoting directly except that you have no quotation marks.

> Raymond Carver writes in one essay that his children were a significant influence on his writing (31).

When referring to an online or electronic source you have a couple of options. There are no page numbers, unless you download a PDF file, so one typically omits this and merely places the last name of the author(s). For clarity, however, you can also refer to the correct paragraph in the text. For example: (Smithart, para. 13).

The Works Cited page is a list of the sources used in your paper and corresponds with the citations in your paper.

What is placed in each entry on your Works Cited page and the order in which it is included depends largely on the type of source that you are using. However, most entries will have certain elements in common. Most will begin with the name of the author or authors. Following the name of the author is the title of the work you are citing. Then you would normally include bibliographic or publication material related to the type of source you are citing.

Certain things must be remembered about the Works Cited page. First of all, it is always the last (and a separate) page(s) of your document and paginated accordingly. Thus, if your essay is five-and-a-half pages long in text, your Works Cited page will be page seven. The words "Works Cited" (without quotation marks) should appear at the top, centered like a title. Like the rest of your paper, this page is double-spaced throughout, with no extra spaces between entries. Each entry after the first is indented five spaces. Your entries should appear in alphabetical order, not the order in which you use them. **All** of the appropriate information about the source should be in the entry. If you are using a source like an article from a journal or magazine or an essay in a collection or anthology, your entry should include all the pages of that entry, not just those you quote from. (Remember that you cite the exact pages you worked from in your internal documentation.)

Note that if more than one city is listed for a book, then you should use only the city that is listed first. You only put the state where a book is published if the city would not be familiar to your readers. In that case, both the city and state are listed. For example: Upper Saddle River, NJ. However, New York and Dallas are known well enough to just include the city. Also, when entering the publisher's name, a shortened form is used. Thus, Harper and Row becomes merely *Harper*, The University of Texas Press becomes *U of Texas P*, and Yale University Press becomes *Yale UP*.

Following are some examples of sources that are used most often on student papers. A more comprehensive look at how to document your sources can be found in *The MLA Guide To Writers of Research Papers* or a good handbook. I also strongly recommend the Purdue Online Writing Lab. Note also that these examples are single-spaced; your Works Cited page is still to be double-spaced.

Sample Entries

A Book

Cohen, Leonard. *Stranger Music: Selected Poems and Songs*. New York: Pantheon, 1993. Print.

Fuller, Randall. *From Battlefields Rising: How the Civil War Transformed American Literature*. New York: Oxford UP, 2011. Print.

A Work in an Anthology or Edited Book

Updike, John. "A & P." *Literature: An Introduction to Reading and Writing*. Ed. Edgar V. Roberts and Henry E. Jacobs. Upper Saddle River, NJ: Prentice, 1998. 316–20. Print.

Tracy, Stephen C. "To the Tune of Those Weary Blues." *Langston Hughes: Critical Perpectives Past and Present* Ed. Henry Louis Gates and K. A. Appiah. New York: Amistad, 1993. 69–93. Print.

An Article in a Magazine

Begley, Sharon, and Sarah Kliff. "The Depressing News about Antidepressants." *Newsweek* 8 Feb. 2010: 34–41. Print.

An Article in a Daily Newspaper

Davis, Kenneth C. "School of Hard Knocks." *New York Times* 26 Dec. 2011: A16. Print.

Solis, Dianne. "Dual Programs Opening Doors." *Dallas Morning News* 26 Feb. 2012: B6+[2]. Print.

A Journal Article (paginated by volume)

Kim, Yeung-Jo, and June-Hee Na. "Effects of Celebrity Athlete Endorsement on Attitude Toward Product: The Role of Credibility, Attractiveness and the Concept of Congruence." *International Journal of Sports Marketing and Sponsorship.* 8.4[3] (2007): 310–320. Print.

An Article Found Using an Online Database

Stewart, Katherine E. "What's Taking Them So Long?" *Chronicle of Higher Education* 20 Mar. 2012: A35. *Academic Search Complete*. Web. 14 May 2012.

Note here that the name of the database is italicized. Also two dates are listed. The first is the date of publication. The second is the date the student accessed the material.

---

[2] The plus sign (+) indicates that the article contains more than one page and that the pages are not continuous.

[3] Here the first number refers to the volume number of the journal and the second to the issue number.

Article from a Website

Allen, Kurt. "'Manchester Choke' Barely Averted In Thrilling Fashion: City Wins First Title in 44 Years." *Midwest Sports Fans*. Midwest Sports Fans 14 May 2012. Web. 15 May 2012.

"Manchester City Win Premier League Title."[4] *Sky News*. Sky.com. 14 May 2012. Web. 15 May 2012.

A Personal Interview

Smithart, Brad. Personal Interview. 12 Sept. 2005.

Keep in mind that one of the most important ways you build credibility with your reader is to pay careful attention to how you document your research. Sloppy or careless documentation does not make an argument invalid or a thesis unlikely. But it can cause a reader to wonder if you, as a writer, have taken your points seriously enough to defend them well. Further, you've worked hard to find this material and to pull it together for your argument. You wouldn't want your good points to be lost in bad writing. So why should your efforts be wasted by poor documentation?

A Note about the Process of Documenting Sources (or why some students get in trouble with plagiarism)

Plagiarism is not so simple as copying something that you did not write and turning it in under your own name. It is not merely about the words one uses, but also about the ideas. It involves giving any impression that material you have in your paper came from your own thoughts and experiences when they did not.

Many students give the impression of cheating because they have been sloppy in their documentation or in the gathering of their research or both. Often the student gathers the books and articles into a big pile, quotes what is needed, and only after the paper has been written, begins to add the internal citations and put together the Works Cited page. Thus, many sources get misquoted or forgotten, and there seem to be gaps between what has been referred to in the essay and what is listed at the end.

But remember that in a very technical sense, any serious error in documentation is plagiarism. While most professors will not fail a research paper for a misplaced comma or a single neglected quote mark, they will also not give you the benefit of the doubt when serious problems have occurred. First, such errors

---

[4] Note that when an author's name is not available, the entry begins with the title of the article.

demonstrate neglect for your reader (and the person who taught you documentation). Second, these problems are easily avoidable.

To avoid plagiarism, one can start by getting in the habit of keeping records of research in the format appropriate for your course. As you find sources, and even before you determine which sources are going to be used in your paper, put them in a working bibliography, and get used to listing those sources in proper MLA format.

Get in the habit of citing the sources internally as you compose your papers. Remember that whether you are quoting directly or paraphrasing, you must cite the source accurately. And since you are typically looking at the source as you write sentences where you refer to it, you should know exactly which source you are citing and insert the correct information. It would be helpful to create the Works Cited page in the original document so you can copy and paste the source information the first time you refer to it in your research paper.

Chapter 4

COMMON SENTENCE-LEVEL WRITING ERRORS

I use the phrase *sentence-level writing* to discuss not only errors in grammar and punctuation, but also issues regarding word choice and style. Most college students who have problems at the sentence level have been making the same mistakes since middle school. The biggest reason for this problem is an inactive approach to writing, where errors have been marked or noted by a teacher and the student has either not learned from those notes or has made required corrections without seeing what is wrong and how to avoid the mistakes in future writing.

Thus, it is important to take an active approach to your sentence-level writing. Many students are rather fatalistic, assuming that the mistakes or problems they have here are just part of "who they are" as writers, but this is not true. Of all the areas of writing, sentence-level errors are among the easiest not only to fix, but to learn from. That is, if they are approached with the right attitude and care.

As noted in Chapter Two, it is vital to actually read notes on your papers and try to understand them. You need to distinguish sentence-level errors from feedback regarding organization and content. You also may need to learn about proofreading marks, which are often used by teachers as a kind of shorthand to mark errors, and how to find information about errors in a handbook. In addition, you should be aware of the errors you make most often, so that on subsequent writing projects you can watch for those specifically, see them in the context of your writing, and work to eliminate them as you learn to write.

Sentence Fragments (frag)

Essentially, a sentence fragment is an incomplete sentence. A complete sentence includes a clear subject and a clear verb or action.

> After my accident. I was more careful about how much I had to drink. (incorrect)
> After my accident, I was more careful about how much I had to drink. (corrected)
> Jan drinks a frozen margarita. Every Friday after work. (incorrect)
> Jan drinks a frozen margarita every Friday after work. (corrected)

Run-Ons (ro) and Comma Splices (cs)

With a run-on, the writer has combined two sentences. A comma splice is like a run-on in that it is two complete sentences. The difference is that a comma separates the two sentences.

> I wanted to go to the concert my parents wouldn't let me. (run-on)
> I wanted to go to the concert, my parents wouldn't let me, (comma splice)
> I wanted to go to the concert, but my parents wouldn't let me. (corrected)
> I wanted to go to the concert. However, my parents wouldn't let me. (corrected)

Wrong Word Errors (ww)

A number of words sound the same but are spelled differently, and thus errors are made when the wrong word is used. Below is a common example.

> to— The word *to* is sometimes a preposition.
>
>> Mark drove us *to the movies.*
>
> The word *to* might be placed in front of a verb to create the infinitive form of the verb.
>
>> I had hoped *to run* in that race.
>
> too— "Too" means also or "in addition."
>
>> Sarah wrote her congressman, *too.*

"Too" can show a great degree of something.

    My friend was *too drunk* to drive home safely.

two— This spelling refers to the number 2.

    I usually drink two cups of coffee before heading to work.

Verb Tense Errors (t)

Verbs are past, present, or future in tense. Writers must use the proper tense for the context of their writing and also be consistent about verb tenses. Sometimes writers accidentally switch tenses in the middle of a piece of writing.

    The crowd *was* really *pumped* up for the show, but the band *disappoint* us. (Note that the second verb in the sentence is in present tense instead of the past tense as it should be.)

Agreement Errors

Agreement, in grammar, is about words that are supposed to go together properly. Subjects must agree in number with their accompanying verbs. That is, singular subjects go with singular forms of the verb, and plural subjects must be put with plural forms of the verb. Pronouns also must agree in number with the nouns they represent.

Subject/verb (s/v agr.)

    Katy drive a truck. (incorrect)

    Katy drives a truck. (agreement)

    We was arguing all night. (incorrect)

    We were arguing all night. (agreement)

Pronouns (pron. agr.)

    Each student must file a degree plan before their junior year. (incorrect)

    Each student must file a degree plan before his or her junior year. (agreement)

    Students must file degree plans before their junior year. (agreement)

Unclear Pronouns (pron.)

A pronoun must be clear about the noun it is referring to. Consider the following examples.

> My dad and my uncle went to college, but he could not finish because he had to work.
>
> This gave me the motivation to keep at it.

In the first sentence, the word "he" could refer to the father or the uncle. In the second, there is nothing clear about what either "this" or "it" refers to.

Quotation Marks (" ")

Quotation marks are used for several different reasons. One is to show what is spoken in dialogue. Place quotation marks around anything spoken by someone, indicating the exact words that have been used. Also, start a new paragraph each time a new person speaks.

> My friend was skeptical. He asked, "Where did you get the money to buy that car?"
>
> "I've been saving twenty percent of my paycheck since last fall," I answered. "Also, my parents matched my savings."

Notice the placement of commas introducing the first quote and the period at the end of the second one.

Quotation marks are also used when reproducing material from research word for word. Remember, you also need a citation to document your research (see Chapter Eight).

Sometimes it becomes necessary to quote something that already has quotation marks around it, such as dialogue. In this case, one would use single quotation marks to indicate the material which is a quote within a quote:

> John asked the professor, "How can we always know when we are in danger of violating the dictum 'First do no harm'?"

Plurals (pl.) and Possession (poss.)

Typically, an "s" or "es" is added to the ends of nouns to make them plural. An apostrophe with an "s" is used to show possession.

> My supervisor's work trucks are always clean and ready to go.

The word *trucks* is plural because there is more than one truck. The person who owns the trucks is the supervisor.

When a noun ends in "s," and you wish to show possession, you merely add an apostrophe:

> My boss' personal car is, however, always dusty on the outside and filled with fast food wrappers on the inside.

Titles

How titles are formatted tells your reader about what kind of work you are referring to. Typically, the title of a long work is italicized. This would mean books, newspapers, magazines, and journal titles. For example, *Newsweek* and *The Dallas Morning News*. Titles of films are also italicized.

Titles of short works are placed in quotation marks. This goes for the tiles of articles in newspapers and magazines, as well song titles and poems. An example might be "Washington Signs Contract Extension for Three Years."

Note that the first letter of each main word is capitalized in all titles. Also, a title and subtitle are separated by a colon. For example: *Wanderlust: A History of Walking* or "Primary Care Screening of Depression and Treatment Engagement in a University Health Center: A Retrospective Analysis."

You will notice that examples in this chapter focus only on common grammar and punctuation problems. I see these as the problems most often in student writing. However, I have not covered matters of style, which are also important. A book I recommend for further reference on both these matters is the classic *Elements of Style* by William Strunk and E. B. White.

Chapter 10

WRITING FOR...

Students justifiably want what they learn in a classroom to be useful to them. When it comes to writing, however, sometimes that practical value is difficult to see until some time has passed and the student is writing on a regular basis in the work world or their personal lives. In addition to what has already been written in *The Active Writer*, let me offer the following suggestions for writing outside the regular English classroom.

Writing for Tests

All writing is stressful in some way, even to those who enjoy it and do it for a living. Writing for tests seems particularly stressful for many reasons. In most cases, one has a limited time to write. Often the student does not even know the question that she or he is expected to respond to. Also, tests tend to carry a great deal of course weight, and the student can't escape the fact that what he or she is doing is important.

Of course, preparation is the key to test taking, but there is more to test taking than study and memorization.

You can prepare for tests by applying the strategies for reading outlined in Chapter Two. Also, notes you take can be the basis of practice writing. You see, while you may not know the exact question you are going to be asked, you should be aware of the subject and many of the pertinent details. You can imagine many sorts of questions and write practice answers to them. This helps you to focus on the material and gets your brain and body used to the unique conditions of test taking. Some students even report to me that writing ahead of time has helped to reduce their test anxiety. They feel more confident because they have been there before.

At the beginning of an essay test, you need read the prompt (or prompts if you are given choices) very carefully. Use the same techniques for reading your test that you would for reading an assignment, noting key directional words.

You may feel the urge to start writing right away, getting as much on paper as possible as quickly as you can. Resist that urge. Usually this results in kind of rhetorical clearing of the throat, where the student merely rambles about the general subject until an idea hits him. By the time that idea comes, the student is tired and almost out of time. Instead, invest a few minutes with a prewriting technique you are comfortable with. Then make a brief plan or outline to follow so that your points are clear and your thoughts organized.

Many times, an essay is only one portion of an exam, often at the end. If this is the case, you should read the essay instructions before working the other sections. You may want to do some prewriting and planning as well. This way the topic has a chance to move around in your mind before you write and you don't have to spend as much time figuring out what to say before you draft as you would if you started the process cold (and tired from the rest of the exam).

Take a couple of minutes to proofread and edit your essay. If your test contains other questions, read through those first, so you can give yourself some distance from your work. Then check for the following:

- Make sure you have a clear thesis early in the essay—in the first paragraph—and that this thesis addresses or answers the question in your prompt. Do not answer a question that has not been asked.
- Each paragraph in the essay should have a point that clearly supports the thesis, and the details in that paragraph (examples, facts, reasoning, etc.) should clearly be connected to that point.
- Sentences should be clear and logical. Proofread for errors you most commonly commit before worrying about a general idea of how it sounds. Keep in mind, also, that abbreviations, informal words and phrases, and emoticons should not be found.

Writing for Other Classes

Every year I am faced with students who honestly believe the only writing they will do is for English classes. Yet, as noted in the first chapter, how well you write will make a difference in many of your grades. You may have fewer writing assignments, and they may not seem all that important, but they are opportunities to learn.

Start early with projects in your other classes and space the work out so that you will have plenty of time to ask needed questions, overcome any hurdles, and make any necessary adjustments. Pay careful attention not only to directions for the assignments, but also what is provided for you in your textbook and class lectures. Often, good ideas for papers and projects can be found there, but students are too busy texting in class to remember what happened.

Focus carefully on the expectations for the assignment, such as the necessity and type of research your teacher wants you to do, and how that research is to be documented. Sometimes students do no research when they were supposed to, too much research, or did not take the time to adequately cite sources.

Remember, professors in other classes may not mark your grammar errors or provide you specific notes about the organization or sentence-level writing of your paper. But that does not mean these elements are less important. Treat each project as professionally and carefully as you expect others to on the job.

Writing in the Work World

Many people approach writing as if every task is the same. Thus, they sometimes find themselves faced with problems when at work trying to write as they "were taught" when the purpose, audience, and context require something a bit different. Others, because they e-mail their bosses or colleagues with the same device they use to text their friends, have a tendency to fill their business correspondence with informal, grammatically baffling sentences that include such non-words as "u," "w/o," and ":-)."

Much of what this book tells you about writing applies to the working world. It is vital to be aware of your purpose, audience, and context. Otherwise, the reader may not even finish looking at what you have to say. However, consider a few differences.

E-mail

- Get to the point early. While you may feel some back story is important, most readers will not be interested or willing to see what all the fuss is about.
- Stick to the main points. Only elaborate as necessary, and be as brief as possible. Most people only have patience for short e-mails. If they want more on a particular subject, they will ask for it.
- As much as possible, leave out emotion. While you may have strong feelings about the subject, an e-mail is rarely the time to express those feelings. Readers are put off by attacks or ranting or gushing, even when they agree with the writer. Above all, NEVER click send when you are angry.

- Do not use informal language and emoticons. Doing so tells your readers you do not care enough about them to use well-constructed language. (This does not mean all e-mails should be stuffy.)
- Proofread carefully and run the spell check if the e-mail is longer than three paragraphs (which should be rare). Again, a lack of care for fixing mistakes tells your reader things about you that you do not want them to think.

Reports, Proposals, Presentations

- Follow the formatting guidelines expected by the company. For coherence sake, the company may expect certain elements of a report to appear in a specific order, or they might want charts or pictures to be a particular size or to be placed in the same place on the page.
- Provide an attention grabbing introduction, but make it brief (unless doing so conflicts with a formatting issue).
- Give only the information that is needed and then move on. Side stories and elaborate examples are likely to get in the way. At the same time, do not let your power point slides do all the talking. No one wants to hear someone read a power point.
- Unless asked for it, your opinion should stay out of it. Of course, when making a proposal or recommendation, you are giving a sort of opinion. But it should be clear to the reader that these points are derived from the facts presented, not your personal feelings.
- Proofread and edit carefully. Many a worker labors intently on a project, only to be embarrassed by typographical errors and grammar mistakes. These tell your readers and viewers that you are sloppy or that you do not care enough about the project to put your best foot forward.

Writing for Yourself

I find I do not have to tell students *how* to write for themselves, but *why* they should. In addition to expressing one's innermost thoughts and dealing with the stresses of life, writing for yourself helps you to organize and develop your ideas for the times they may need to be shared with others. Sometimes when students have too much of an emotional investment in the subject matter, I recommend writing those feelings down so they can build some distance from the material. That way when the real assignment comes, the student can focus on the purpose and not let emotions cloud their ability to look honestly and fairly about the subject.

Another very important reason to cultivate the habit of writing each day (or at least regularly) is that the act of writing anything is good practice. It exercises your mind and body—yes writing is also a physical activity—in the same way stretching and running prepare an athlete for the rigors of a game.

Consider the following activities:

- Keep a journal or diary of your daily thoughts or activities.
- Start a notebook that chronicles what you learn in your classes each week.
- Start a blog about an activity or hobby that interests you.
- Write letters you never send. You can write a famous figure from the past or someone in the future.
- Take issues or problems or controversies connected with your major and write proposals for how to fix or improve things.
- Think about arguments you have had and write down the dialogue you wish had taken place. If you are anticipating an argument, consider writing out the dialogue you expect to take place.
- Write character sketches of people you know, but do not know well. Describe them with as much detail as you can remember.
- Write a poem or short story about a recent situation. Explore how the events or feelings could have been different or more interesting.
- Imagine something you have to do at work and try to come up with a better method or way to make the task more fun.
- Take something you have written for a class or work and rewrite it from a perspective other than your own, such as a classmate or your boss.

Not everyone is called upon to be a poet, and such activities may feel uncomfortable at first, but long after your college career is over you will realize that writing was not so much about talent or ability, but about practice and tapping into the potential that exists for everyone who encounters language.

Appendix

FORMS

Syllabus Contract

After carefully reading the syllabus for this class, ask your professor any questions about policies and information that you do not understand. Then fill out, sign, and date the form below.

I, _____, have read the course syllabus, and I am familiar with the basic policies, procedures, and rules of the class.

_____
(your name)

_____
Date

Reading Quizzes

All questions should be answered in complete paragraphs with correctly written sentences. Specific references to the book should be noted in proper MLA format using the page number in parentheses at the end of the sentence and quotation marks around directly quoted material.

Chapter 1

1. Why should students want to be better writers?
2. What is the difference between competence and just getting by?
3. What is active writing?
4. Explain what a student can do, even without taking an English class, to improve his/her writing.
5. What does it mean to be a "one-draft wonder"?

Chapter 2

1. Explain why students, according to the author, are not active readers.
2. Name and describe the steps of active reading.
3. Summarize the section of the chapter "Reading Your Assignments."
4. Summarize the section of the chapter "Reading Your Teacher's Feedback."
5. Explain why a student should read her/his syllabus carefully.

Chapter 3

1. Explain the different purposes one might have for writing.
2. Summarize the main ideas of the section on audience.
3. Define *context* and explain its importance to each writing project.
4. Define *thesis* and explain why writers should make theirs specific and clear, noting as well what to avoid when composing thesis statements.
5. Explain at least three methods of development in your own words.

Chapter 4

1. Define *prewriting*, and explain how it helps students.
2. Summarize the material in the chapter about distractions and preparation.
3. Describe the forms of outlines.
4. Describe the various rough draft forms.
5. What significant points does the chapter make about introductions and conclusions?

6. Explain the three ways a reader "sees" a piece of writing.
7. Explain the focus of the first stage of revision, noting the questions one should ask about one's writing.
8. Explain, in your own words, the questions one should ask in the stage of revision where one focuses on individual paragraphs.
9. Explain, in your own words, what one should do during the stage where one sharpens sentences and words.
10. Summarize the sections "Peer Review" and "Other Ideas for Improving Your Writing."

Chapter 5

1. Explain what development strategies are.
2. Summarize, in your own words, the section on narration and description.
3. Summarize, in your own words, the section on comparison and contrast.
4. Summarize, in your own words, the section on process.
5. Summarize, in your own words, the section on examples.
6. Summarize, in your own words, the section on cause and effect.
7. Summarize, in your own words, the section on classification, division, and definition.
8. Summarize, in your own words, the section on argument.
9. Explain how a writer might use more than one developmental strategy in a single essay.
10. Pick one developmental strategy and explain how you have used it in non-academic writing.

Chapter 6

1. Explain why the active writer should not consider an argument merely a conflict to overcome or a competition.
2. What does the chapter tell us about how academic writers should see argument?
3. Explain the basic parts of the argument.
4. What are appeals, and how do they work in a good argument?
5. Define "logical fallacies" and explain two examples.

Chapter 7

1. Explain common misconceptions about research (Research is not...).
2. Summarize the section "Some ideas for gathering information."
3. Explain what the text tells us about how to tell if a source might be useful.

4. Summarize the section "Checking Reliability/Credibility."
5. Summarize the information about writing the research paper, including notes on revision.

Chapter 8

1. Explain, in your own words, why it is important to document research.
2. Explain what in-text, or parenthetical, citations are.
3. Explain what the Works Cited page is and note what must be included on that page.
4. Looking over the sample entries in the chapter, and explain what is common to each Works Cited page entry.
5. Explain what plagiarism is and what the text suggests in order to avoid it.

Chapter 9

1. What are sentence-level errors, and why do students continue to make them?
2. Explain what sentence fragments are and how to fix them.
3. Explain what comma splices and run-on sentences are, and explain how to fix them.
4. What are agreement errors?
5. Explain unclear pronoun errors.
6. Explain verb tense errors.
7. Explain the proper ways to use quotation marks.
8. Summarize the errors concerned with plural words and possessive words.
9. In your own words, explain the proper way to punctuate titles.
10. Explain what sentence-level error you make most often and what you will do to eliminate it in the future.

Chapter 10

1. Summarize the strategies you can use to prepare for tests.
2. Summarize what the text tells us about what to check for after writing a draft of an essay test.
3. Summarize, in your own words, the section "Writing for Other Classes."
4. Summarize, in your own words, the section "Writing for the Work World."
5. Explain what the text tells us about the value of writing for oneself, highlighting how you can use one of the examples.

9. As you review the essay, carefully check the format of quotations and other references to outside sources. Give an example of one that seems incorrect. This is very important.

10. Give two strengths you found in this essay.

    a.

    b.

11. Give two suggestions for improvement. If you need ideas about what to suggest, think about what's not clear or look at the questions in the revision section of Chapter Four.

    a.

    b.

Writer/Title:_____   Reader: _____

Workshop Form #3

Read the paper all the way through. Make notes on the following. Return the notes to the writer. When you get your notes, write them down on your own copy. Turn one copy in to the instructor. You may use the back if necessary.

_____   _____
Student writer   Reader

Write the thesis statement: _____

_____

_____

Does the thesis match what is expected in the assignment? (Circle one)

                Yes   No   I don't know.

Is this thesis clear? Is it specific and focused? What would make this thesis clearer?

Does each body paragraph support or develop the thesis? Note the paragraph numbers that do not develop the thesis clearly (even if you are not sure). What is needed?

Note body paragraphs (by number) where main points, material from the poem or story, research, and other developing material are not clearly connected. That is, if you have trouble following anything, note the paragraph and explain the problem as thoroughly as you can.

Appendix Workshop Form #3

Note below where anything that does not come from the writer is not properly cited within the essay. (Stop at five examples.)

Check that everything in the Works Cited page is referred to in the essay. Note that each in-text citation has a corresponding entry on the Works Cited page. Note below any errors on the Works Cited page.

Note below example of up to three different errors in sentence-level writing.

What other work do you think the writer needs to do in revising this essay?